Where I Am From

Student Affairs Practice from the Whole of Students' Lives

Susan E. Borrego and Kathleen Manning

and NASPA's 2002–2005

Minority Undergraduate Fellows Program (MUFP) Fellows

Adam-Jon Aparicio, Nicolas Los Baños, Jessica Barron, Akirah Jerelle Bradley,
Natalie M. Byrdsong, Devetta Blackman, Randall P. Bogard, Aeza Mae Bolo,
Lesley-Ann Brown, Sarah M. Childs, Peter Chu, Jessie Cordova, Jose Castillo, Katie Curiel,
Joseph "Piko" Ewoodzie, Sterling Garcia, Cameron J. Harris, Ivania Hernandez,
Susana Hernandez, Denise Herrera, Kimberly Herrera, J. V. Hollenbeck, Rebecca Hossain,
Briza Juarez, E. K. Lewis, Charmaine Lastimoco, Luana Mona, Tiarra Netter, Julie J. Park,
Cynthia Payne, Aretha M. Perry, Candace Nikki Rogers, Darrell A. Rodriguez,
Kassandra Rodriguez, Marie Smallwood, Davida S. Smith, LaTasha Smith,
Karlen N. Suga, Adiam Tesfay, Rouel Garingo Velasco, Andrew Villanueva, Todd Wilcox

NASPA
Student Affairs Administrators
in Higher Education

Contents

Acknowledgments

No one gets to the place of producing a book on his or her own. The work is often the result of years of conversations and interactions that ultimately lead to the published piece. This book is truly that. I am grateful to the colleagues, students, and professionals that have interacted with me through time in ways that shape my daily practice. I am especially grateful to the MUFP fellows who chose to share themselves through these narratives and for what we were able to learn together and to NASPA for providing the venue.

–Susan E. Borrego

I give thanks to all the people of color who took me under their wings and brought me up. They tutored, encouraged, and confronted me over the years in such generous ways. I feel so honored to have been given the gift of opened eyes.

–Kathleen Manning

Foreword

Adam-Jon Aparicio and Akirah Jerelle Bradley

Minority Undergraduate Fellowship Program (MUFP) Alumni
and Higher Education and Student Affairs Administration Masters Students

The experiences of students of color at predominately White institutions are multi-layered with adversity, challenge, and promise. We are two graduate students engaged in the design of helping the students we supervise and mentor develop a positive identity through acknowledging their individual experiences. As students and young professionals of color we often struggle to find a place where our voices are truly heard. Despite the refusal of many on predominantly White campuses to hear our unique perspectives, ideas, and needs, we persevere in using our voices and supporting our students to use theirs. We will continue to do so until our voices are respected and included in the majority.

We are two of more than 40 authors in the "Where I Am From" Minority Undergraduate Fellows Program (MUFP) fellows' narratives you will read in this book. These stories are rich, revealing, and true as they poetically commemorate our diverse experiences. We invite you to get a deeper view into our journey of becoming fellows in this remarkable program. In addition to showing the readers where the fellows come from, we take this opportunity to shine light on where we are going. As fellows, we recognize that our many experiences have the ability to influence the way we move through the world *and* the field of student affairs. As future professionals we rejoice in the memories of the struggles we have overcome and the vision we have for the future.

Meaningful Connections in Student Affairs

My name is Akirah Jerelle Bradley and I am a MUFP alumna who began my journey as a fellow in 2003 at Mansfield University of Pennsylvania as a student intern to the vice president of student affairs. There I became intrigued with the field of student affairs and knew that I wanted to pursue an advanced degree to make a difference in the field by generating a healthier environment for underrepresented students.

The deeper I got into the profession the more I noticed that I was one of few people of color in this profession. As I read about the history of student affairs, culture of higher education, and theories of student development I found that there was a deeper meaning of connection missing in this field. I knew that I was not alone because many of the MUFP fellows I met over the years expressed the same sentiment.

The program provided me with a mentor who understood my struggle and guided me through the process of creating a stronger identity. I earnestly believe that students are more successful when they have mentors and/or individuals who support them. I don't think I would have survived my undergraduate career if it were not for the women who consistently empowered me through the years. Through the deeds of these student affairs professionals I found a sense of belonging in the field of student affairs.

Observing and learning from my mentors allowed me to reach into my heart and find passion for the work I did as a student leader and do now as a new practitioner. My goal is to empower students by returning the love and support that I received as an undergraduate student. When meaningful connection and inclusiveness are incorporated into the student affairs profession, continuous learning, change, and advancement follow.

INCLUSION, MENTORSHIP, AND EMPOWERMENT

My name is Adam-Jon Aparicio. My MUFP experience began when a student affairs practitioner asked me if I had ever considered a career in students affairs. Like many fellows before me, I replied with, "What's student affairs? You mean I can get paid to do this stuff?" Being a first generation college student I knew little about opportunities in graduate studies and never truly thought that I was capable of continuing my education past the undergraduate level. When I applied and was accepted to be a MUFP fellow in 2003, I began to entertain the idea of furthering my education through a graduate degree in a field that fused my passion for identity development, community involvement, and social justice with my love for the university environment. It was through my MUFP experience that I began to realize that my future wasn't limited and I had people who were truly invested in my educational and professional life.

MUFP fellows are charged with providing their universities with a project that benefits underrepresented students as well as upholds values of inclusion and mentorship within student affairs and higher education. My project, developed with the guidance of my mentors, Nancy Moonhee Cha and Andrea Monroe, was a conference that educated undergraduates of color about the many graduate opportunities within student affairs. The Higher Education and Student Affairs (HESA) Graduate School Conference was held at my alma mater, the University of California, Santa Cruz, and welcomed more than 40 students to learn about the field of student affairs and the opportunities that graduate school can provide. The HESA Conference was honored to have such influential practitioners and faculty members involved: Dr. Robert Kelly and Dr. Jacob Diaz (Seattle University), Dr. Kristen Renn (Michigan State University), Dr. Bridget Turner Kelly (Seattle University), and Dr. Kim West (University of Southern California).

It was through this experience that I truly felt like I was meant to work within higher education. There I was, a gay, Latino, first-generation college student from a low-income family (an underrepresented student in many ways) and people valued the work I was doing, nationally. I was empowered and felt like I could truly make a significant contribution to the field of student affairs. Being a MUFP fellow not only opened the doors to further my education, it broke down the walls of adversity that many people of color before me had to face to be respected in this field. My MUFP experience is responsible for the practitioner I am today and for the greatness I can inspire in other students of color throughout my career.

APPRECIATION FOR THE BOOK

A mission of this book is to provide a forum for the narratives of students of color to be heard and recognized as real, valid, and vital aspects of diverse and inclusive institutions of higher education. As graduate students of color we navigate the field of student affairs with underrepresented identities. We understand the importance of sharing our own voices in order to mentor the undergraduates with whom we work. This book provides us with two opportunities to highlight the importance of racial and ethnic diversity by (1) publishing the narratives we created as undergraduates to examine our experiences as students of color and (2) engaging us as current practitioners whose narratives are now more informed by issues of student development.

We are extremely thankful for this book as it provides a framework of validation, understanding, and support by providing MUFP fellows with a platform to be heard. The authors of this book, Drs. Susan Borrego and Kathleen Manning, continue to work toward establishing a pedagogy that inserts soul into education. The soul is found at the heart of education when there is true representation and expression of cultural diversity. There are many books that discuss theories without being cognizant of the voices or experiences that are not included. The fellows in this book are inviting readers to listen to their truth by way of the "Where I Am From" narratives.

Just as the telling narratives express, many students of color have always had a voice that espouses their inner thoughts, struggles, and frustrations with being a marginalized group. However, the voices of students of color are seldom heard in the literature or represented in the higher education theories. This book encourages these students to truthfully provide voice to their experiences and it implores practitioners to regard these voices as fuel for change.

In this book, Borrego and Manning have essentially introduced the MUFP fellows as indispensable members of the field and as change agents working toward the eradication of discriminative practices within all of higher education. It is through their narratives that these students explore their true voices. The outcome is a series of exploration of students' lives that are raw, real, and powerful. As true participants of this book, the MUFP fellows are not merely being examined; they are delivering their whole selves, complete with the good, bad, negative, unique, meaningful, and amazing. These fellows are speaking up and staunchly challenging practitioners to listen with hope that higher education can change for the better.

Borrego and Manning deliver a framework that empowers students of color to use their voice to move past people's negative assumptions. Moreover, the fellows' narratives expose the Du Boisian idea of double consciousness which states that for many students of color navigating the university experience (which in many cases operates within White culture) two realities are created. W.E.B. Du Bois (1969) stated that double consciousness describes an individual whose identity has two separate, contradictory identities. In order for practitioners to understand this double consciousness, they must understand that students of color operate in both a world dominated by White culture (e.g., predominantly White institutions) as well as in the reality of their own racial and ethnic upbringing. Providing this framework here ensures that the voices of students of color are not only being heard, but intentionally explored to create better pedagogical practices for working with students. Borrego and Manning challenge practitioners to adopt practices that are grounded in the experiences of students of color.

We see this book as a definitive example of the power that students of color possess to create a more inclusive field. The MUFP fellows who participated in this book's production gave Borrego and Manning permission to peer into our narratives and to publish them for the student affairs audience. We gave our consent to allow the authors to think about the experiences of students of color and decipher ways in which practitioners can truly provide more conscious and inclusive services to all students.

THANK YOU TO THE FELLOWS

We express our gratitude to all the fellows. The perspectives that fellows bring to the profession are valuable beyond measure and their presence alone can initiate change. Unfortunately, this presence does not come without cost. When people of color use their voices to display who they are, where they come from, and where they are going, they will innately challenge the negative assumptions that others may have developed about them. Audre Lorde (2003) aptly stated, "I have come to believe over and over again that what is most important to me must be spoken, made verbal and shared, even at the risk of having it bruised or misunderstood" (p. 64). It is important and necessary for MUFP students to share their authentic voices to create change in higher education.

Thank you to the MUFP fellows for submitting your personal reflections through the "Where I Am From" narratives. These future practitioners expressed their truth and revealed hidden identities to the world. Through their narratives, the fellows poured their souls into the reader's hands. We acknowledge their courage and are grateful for the leadership they display in initiating change by using their voices and the power of their words. These narratives are the foundation of a pedagogy that incorporates inclusiveness for all students of color as they (we) navigate through institutions of higher learning.

January 2007

REFERENCES

Du Bois, W. E. B. (1969). *The Souls of Black Folk.* New York: Penguin Inc.

Lorde, A. (2003). (5th ed). Age, race, class, and sex: Women redefining difference. In M. L. Anderson. *Race, class, and gender: An anthology.* Boston: Wadsworth Publishing

Introduction

Voices of the Minority Undergraduate Fellows Program (MUFP) Fellows

I am my own story.
The right to say I am from where I am
and have the last word
Because I'm the only one who can answer that question.
–Julie J. Park

The concept of "voice" is much discussed in higher education. In academic circles—in every discipline and every program—how to exercise and express one's voice is an issue. This book is about voice, especially underrepresented students' voices rarely heard in colleges and universities or in student affairs literature and research. It is not that these voices are not present; rather, they are more likely ignored or misinterpreted. When present, some on college and university campuses dismiss their relevance. Some find their cadence or tone difficult to understand. But not having a voice at the table or not having it represented in "official" places such as literature or policy does not mean that someone does not have a voice. This book is a medium for voices. It is a testament to the idea that students—especially students of color (given the history of higher education)—have the right to define themselves.

The book presents the voices of students in NASPA's Minority Undergraduate Fellows Program (MUFP). The program was established in 1987 to encourage the number of minority students in higher education and student affairs. Since its early founding, the population of students served was expanded to include gay, lesbian, bisexual, and transgender students and students with disabilities. In 2005, the program's name was changed to the NASPA Undergraduate Fellows Program (NUFP) to reflect the wider audience served. In this book, the authors refer to the program as the Minority Undergraduate Fellows Program or MUFP, which was the name in effect when the narratives were written. All narratives were written by students of color although some fellows were students with disabilities and others were gay, lesbian, bisexual, or transgender. In no way, however, are the narratives or the interpretations offered meant to represent *all* students of color.

The fellows included in this book participated in the Summer Leadership Institute (SLI) and took part in an exercise called "Where I Am From." Through the exercise, Susan Borrego attempted to bring the idea of scholarship into the SLI but, more importantly, encouraged the students to give voice to their experiences. Borrego and the SLI faculty understood that students had a right to define themselves; a right often denied to students of color. "Where I Am From" was an opportunity to ground the SLI participants in their pasts and their own experiences as they attended college. The exercise helped them understand that their experiences matter and are important to creating a more complete learning environment. This was an important message to convey to the fellows because their experiences are often rendered invisible on college campuses.

> I am an uncertain, beat up, exhausted black girl hiding behind the mask of a strong, powerful,
> educated, self-empowered,
> and self-motivated black women.
> –Lesley-Ann Brown

As first proposed by Borrego, the "Where I Am From" exercise was a risk because it asked students of color to expose parts of themselves often kept hidden. Borrego had been introduced to the exercise herself in a writing workshop facilitated by a poet. Because the starting point is the students' experience, Borrego connected it to David Kolb's experiential learning theories (1984). She explained Kolb's model to the MUFP fellows in the following terms. First, you have an experience. Then you reflect on that experience by asking, for example, "What makes it different or the same as…?" Next, you test what you learned from the experience in a new situation and reflect on how it worked in that situation. Then you consider how you will apply what you've learned to your environment. Borrego used Kolb as a way to teach students to experience, reflect, and question. She assured the MUFP fellows that each of them had meaningful experiences, and encouraged them to reflect on those experiences and see what questions arose, even if they felt lost and doubtful about saying anything of value. Finally, she brought them to the action-based question: "So, what do you do...?"

In this way, they see that their experiences have meaning and are a source of knowledge and understanding. Borrego wanted the fellows to recognize that they brought important experiences to higher education. The exercise provided them with a way to connect their personal experiences with the experiences that they would have in college—to ground them in their own experiences. It encouraged them to express and understand what it means to be who you are in a place often inhospitable to that concept, and to realize that they could use the knowledge gained from their experiences to sustain them in college.

Students of color, adult students, and working-class or poor students often feel excluded in higher education settings. The theories, methods of conducting business, and spoken and unspoken rules of college and university life differ from the places from which many of these students come. The "Where I Am From" narratives in this book are a window into the experiences of students not well represented in the theories and practices that guide work in higher education and student affairs. The purpose of this book is to broaden perspectives, encourage learning, and expand the reader's response repertoire. We hope to convey the need to listen to and talk about what students of color say about themselves—not what the theory says or neglects to say about them. A guiding principle of the exercise is that if we, the educators, can get out of the way, then students will fill their rightful space and express their feelings. We must get out of the way and avoid the inclination to privilege our forms, experiences, or assumptions over those of students. Education is about respecting and honoring the voices of students and their means of expression.

"Where I Am From" created an opportunity for the expression of voice in ways that open the academy to a diversity of perspectives. When you read these narratives, you'll be amazed at how poetic they are, although the fellows were not asked to write poetry. They were simply read two samples of previous "Where I Am From" narratives and asked to write their own. They were encouraged to believe that they had something important to say; that their experiences were important, worth writing about, and central to the practice of higher education.

> *I'm from the bond we discovered between us*
> *and the struggle we took to get there.*
> *–Joseph Piko Ewoodzie*

We, Susan Borrego and Kathleen Manning, are two White women from working class families. Like many people who work in higher education, we straddle class-consciousness. What we have in common with the fellows who wrote the narratives in this book is the feeling that we are in a place not designed for us. Somewhere, somehow, we were given the opportunity for education; we live and work in places where family members, former schoolmates, and others from our past seldom went. While we may not share a common experience of race with many of the "Where I Am From" authors, we do share the common experience of being outsiders in the academy.

We take our role as stewards of and witnesses to the book very seriously. The narratives express private thoughts, experiences, and dreams. We worried about our ability to convey the legacy of these voices. At the same time, we understand that it is not our role to paternalistically protect the fellows, who are quite capable of protecting themselves. In fact, all the students gave permission to have their narratives published in this book. We agonized that our privilege (e.g., race, education, class, professional status) gave us the opportunity to publish a book including their voices—a chance that they, most likely, would not be offered. We worried that our degrees in student affairs and higher education had created a distance from our immediate experience—that we had been "trained away" from it. There is something about education that can break you or strip you down to become something you are not. Even now, we worry that our summaries of the narrative themes do not do justice to the sentiments and passion expressed in these narratives. Most of all, we worry that both student and racial identity development theory do not recognize the assets that students of color, like the MUFP fellows, possess.

> *Persistence to prove I could do*
> *more than others believed.*
> *Fear and overcoming it from*
> *hope and pride and endurance.*
> *—Briza Juarez*

The original purpose of the "Where I Am From" exercise was to give the fellows an opportunity to express their voices as well as connect them to the process of scholarship and education. We did not plan to write a book or develop a theory from the narratives. Yet after several years of conducting the exercise, Borrego realized that the narratives warranted a wider audience. They show that students are so much more than we know and that their experiences are so much deeper and richer than theory suggests. The voices expressed in the narratives reveal the ways and places where "messiness" is the order of the day and where interesting substance happens at the borders and boundaries of experience.

ORGANIZATION OF THE BOOK

The first half of the book contains the MUFP fellows' narratives. They are loosely arranged by theme, but you will probably read into and interpret your own themes from the narratives. There are multiple themes that overlap, double back, and repeat in an iterative, not logical, fashion. In the second half of the book, we, Borrego and Manning, summarize and discuss the themes that we interpreted from the narratives. We relate the themes to student affairs practice and theory but, more importantly, we discuss the theory grounded in the narratives. Our goal is to let the narratives speak for themselves—as authentic expressions of their experiences. We believe that the narratives speak to a whole that is often missing from the professional literature.

References

Kolb, D.A. (1984). *Experiential learning: Experience as the source of learning and development.* Englewood Cliffs, NJ: Prentice Hall.

PART I

Narratives of Students in the Minority Undergraduate Fellows Program

CHAPTER 1

Family, Neighborhoods, Love, Disappointment, and History

Where I Am From

J. V. Hollenbeck

I am from the land of the Midnight Sun
Of coffee beans and sourdough pancakes
Of fresh off the boat and yellow produce
Of Nordstroms and Wal-Mart
Of "Before It was a State"
  and "I Got Stationed Here"

Where a Broadway show has equal precedence
   with attending the State Fair
A place of alcohol and misspent youth
Where rural meets urban in a sandpaper
   kind of way—she flew back to the village
Carharts with Doc Martens and prom dresses from
   Seattle

Culture and independence shake hands while
   the world's harsh reality kicks you in the tail
Beauty and peace are the shore that
   meet the sea of unrest and the mountains
   asking to be moved with faith and a little time
   border every day and when there is no night
Nature fosters learning but slightly warps time

But time is such a lower 48 thing as are
   our MTV dreams and credit card desires

All in all, Alaska is and always will be home.

Where I Am From

Todd Wilcox

I am from a place that makes me the person I am today. I'm from a place of simplicity and humble beginnings.

I am Salt Clan, born for San Juan Pueblo, my maternal grandparents

2

are Towering House Clan, and my paternal grandparents are Edgewater Clan.

Ashiihi nishli. Kinlichiinii Dine'e bashishchiin. Kiya'aanii da' shicheii. Tabaaha' da' shinali.

This is my identity as a Navajo man from the communities of Leupp and Winslow, Arizona.

I am from my experiences as a little rez boy growing up in the boonies with my parents, one brother, and four sisters.

I am from my mother's love, my father's strength, and my Grandmother's wisdom and happiness.

I am from a place where playing basketball and volleyball were my escape and where past trips to town on the weekends were spent visiting family, grocery shopping, and a hopeful trip to McDonalds.

I am from a place where fried potatoes and tortillas is a delicacy, and the aroma of frybread grease and mutton stew from a local vendor can be welcoming.

I am from a history of the Long Walk, government policy, cultural assimilation, relocation, boarding school education, and broken promises.

I am from love and family, struggle and sacrifice, culture and tradition, education and achievement.

This is me, this is my way of life. This is where I am from.

Where I Am From

Aeza Mae Bolo

I am from here and there, and every where; but mainly I am from a land filled with sun, tourist, coconut trees, exotic flowers and crashing waves on the south shore. Even bikinis and surf shorts all around.

I am from military boots, fatigues, PX's commissaries and military life. I am from structure that has made me into the person that I am today. I am from obedience and military time, moving here and there. From new friends made and old ones that may seem lost, but are just at a distance. I am from love and laughter all around me, never ending as the world revolves around. Strong family ties that bond me to my blood.

I am from busy-hustling days on campus that students flock to. The busy days and nights, so that I can keep myself occupied. Busy days of meetings, classes, work, and more work—just so that I can keep myself occupied. Days when I sleep at midnight and wake up at 4:00 a.m. The craziness that everyday life brings upon each person. I can handle!!! But sometimes I think I can be super woman.

I am from the quietness and peacefulness that the world cares for. The silence that you hear on street corners at one in the morning. I am from romance and love that floats in the air when he is nearby. I am from the softness of the feathered-down pillow that I lay on at night, the softness that soothes your soul when times are rough. I am from the light feather or the soft petal that falls as the wind breezes through. I am me...I am Aeza.

Where I Am From

Darrell A. Rodriguez

I am from the country—where kids play outside all day and eat fresh peaches from the trees. I am from the ghetto—where crack heads walk the streets and gunshots are normal. I am from a culture rich in tradition, with large festivals, music, and tortillas. I am from a culture centered around family and hard work, with cornbread, apple pie, and country music. I'm from a family of cotton pickers who came from the hills of Tennessee. I am from faith, work, and dreams. I am from no money. I am from scratch. I am from nothing. I am from setbacks, slow progress, and low pay. I am the underdog that was kicked and then asked why don't you have anything? I am from hope for a better tomorrow and the promise of a brand new day. I am the dream.

Where I Am From

Kimberly Herrera

Where I am from family is very important. As you would say in Hawaii, Ohana is all around you.
Where I am from there is all kinds of noise from the taxi drivers honking, babies crying to the little hoodlums in the corner by the bodega whistling at the pretty girls passing by.

Where I am from the most important seasonings used in food are Adobo and Sazon. My friends laugh at me because I put those two specific seasonings in everything I make from rice & beans to spaghetti.

Where I Am From

No matter what social event is going on you always see the same people in the neighborhood. The little girls playing jump rope, the guys playing dominoes, the women gossiping about what's going on in the neighborhood and, last but not least, the abuelitas in the kitchen cooking and preparing food.

I didn't grow up in New York City all my life but it is always home for me. When I take a ride into the city I end up doing the same routine. I take the train to my grandfather's restaurant, get food for my grandmother and I such as arroz y gondules, white rice with caldito, pollo guisado, pernil, and of course pan con mantequilla.

As I am walking home, I buy some batteries from a guy selling them off the street.

Oh wait, where is the guy with the coco???? As I pass the bodega, I see the little boys in the neighborhood and how they are growing up to be men but still doing the same things with their lives, hanging out on the block.

But of course, they know me as the college girl. As I walk into my grandmother's building I see the neighborhood gossip Jackie shrinking from drugs and I see my cousin with a face full of makeup wishing she were 25.

But I laugh to myself because this is what I see and expect every time I go home.

I walk into my grandmother's apartment and ask her for her blessing and she tells me "Que dios te bendiga."

We eat and I speak to her in Spanglish, both English and Spanish. I feel right at home. This is where I'm from.

You probably are all saying "Well why is she telling us her routine of when she goes to the city."

This routine is where I come from: My culture, my life, and the things that I love.

Who I Am, Where I Am From

Peter Chu

I am from a place where there were locked doors and closed minds.

But a father and mother who always said "in time." Hey—father and mother, can you feel that separation? I did, in an instant, there was no preparation. "But you will make it someday, you will get there," were the echoes that raced through my mind from my brother and sister's care. I am from a place, where some of you call home, except I didn't call it that, I called it alone. Everything happens for a reason, that's what I always say. Put your life in God's hands, just drop to your knees and pray. "As I lay me down to sleep I pray the Lord my soul to keep, if I should die before I wake....Thank you."

Why? Why would someone say this, you ask? Well from a life of pain and sorrow, poems and songs trying to figure out why everything was going wrong. Walking around with my head hung low, even got to the point where I didn't want to go. And that was it, I was done. Once you hit rock bottom, there's no where left to go...but up. "Smack"—the sound of my sisters hand across my face. Hypothetically of course, but it still left a trace. "What are you doing?" she said, "we'll get through this together. We've been through bad times, but the sun will shine through the weather." One hundred and eighty degrees, I call it my 2nd turn around. Helping others find themselves, and helping me learn. So now whenever I question myself and feel ever so lost, I turn to my favorite line by Robert Frost. Yet still the way it was written was not enough, I took his line, revamped it and made my own verse. "Two roads diverged in the woods, I took the one less traveled, made my own path, so I can find my way back to help others. So I'll tell you who I am and where I am from—the road less traveled is where it all began."

Where I Am From

Marie Smallwood

I am a person that's looked up to, not only by my little sister, but by my whole family. I'm a person that's put on a tall pedestal, but always trying to get down. I'm southern and country to the people that don't live in the south, but sound like "a white girl" to the people that lives around me. I live in someone else's dream. I'm the one that's going to make it, but what is it? Then it might not be my it. I don't even know my own dreams because I live the life that everyone wants me to live so I convinced myself that's what I want. I get depressed because I don't really know who I am. I am so wrapped up in what I'm supposed to do that I don't think about self. They tell me that I'm a "strong black woman," but what does that really mean?

Where I Am From

Natalie M. Byrdsong

I am from Red and Blue flashing lights
And sirens blaring through the night
From the days it was safe and ok
To play hide and go seek outside
But be in by the time the streetlights came on.

From a place where love is a fantasy but also
A safety net
Where the biggest smile might shield away
The times of sadness, disappointment and despair.

Friends who are far and in between
And the ones you trust—you never try to let go
Music of Marvin Gaye; Donny Hathaway and
Stevie Wonder that brings you to deep thought,
But eases your soul.

I lived in the world of Street Dreams
Where things can go beyond the limit of the sky
But quick $$$, too many babies, and a quick high
Make the boundaries harder and the people forget
About the ride.

A place of solitude, a hope of joy, and
A peace of mind are the elements
That pushed me forward and a way to escape
Towards my own destiny.

Where I Am From

Davida S. Smith

West side of Chicago
Rough looking on the outside
Much love and respect on the inside
Neighbors looking out for me as I walk to and from
  school

I am from a Preacher and Missionary's home
Monday night prayer, Tuesday night bible class, Friday
  night Weekly service
Saturday rehearsal and Sunday morning services
This describes my weeks as a young one.

I saw my parents attend church and laugh and smile
  with people
Once home, that love and sincerity didn't change.
They showed love and respect to everyone.
It was nothing unusual for someone to call late in the
Midnight hour asking for prayer.
Or to have someone come and stay with us in our
  one bedroom

*Apartment until they were able to get back on their
    feet.*

*I am from a home of respect and obedience
Not only did I have to mind at home, but also in
    church,
school, grocery store etc…
There were no harsh words or yelling to keep me in
    line
Simply a stern look and the fear of momma's purse
    strap being
Transformed into her "Special Helper" and hearing
    her say "do
I need to get my help?"*

*I am from a home that firmly believed and relied on
"The Lord shall supply all of my needs…"
I never heard or saw complaint,
Just praise to God and the result of that praise.*

*I come from "Do unto others as you would want
    them to do to you,"
"Be your own person"
"Always Think!"
"Education is the key to go places."
"Never limit yourself or allow anyone else to limit
    you."*

*I am from a southern belle of a mom
Frozen dinners? Canned foods?*

Those were unknown in our home.
Collard greens, baked macaroni and cheese, smothered pork
chops or chicken, homemade cornbread (not jiffy), southern
style biscuits (not pillsbury), candied yams (with or without
marshmallows), potato salad, mustard and turnip greens
(ham hock included), pound cakes, 3 layered caramel and
Chocolate cakes (homemade icings), lemon meringue pie,
Sweet potato pie and kool aid.
That's where I'm from

Where I Am From

Joseph "Piko" Ewoodzie

I'm from a land far, far away stored in my heart of memories. I'm from uncertainties because when I'm asked where I'm from, I usually ask...what do you mean?

I'm from Monrovia, Liberia, where my family fled at time of war. I'm from Gomoa Jukwa, Gomoa Ankamm, Agona Sweden where I was introduced to life as I know it.

I'm from the tears that I shed when I said goodbye to my mother to come to this new land. I'm from the joy that filled me when coming here gave me a chance to get to know an absent dad. I'm from the bond we discovered between us and the struggle it took to get there. I'm from the depth of misunderstood and misguided love that lives in my home. I'm from the strict rules that broke my spirit only to be rebuilt. I'm from the love of education that lived in my home. I'm from essays, books, and articles that my dad left on my desk to read, just for conversations while we make pancakes on Saturday morning.

To tell you the truth, I often do not know where I'm from. But every word, every action, every experience have molded who I am, and it stays in my heart.

I'm from love.

I'm from helping and being helped.

CHAPTER 2

Multi-culturalism, Multi-lingualism, Identity, and...

Where I Am From

Adam-Jon Aparicio

When I look at myself in the mirror, I see myself in shades. Much like shades of color, my shades come in identities. My identities allow me to understand me. They help paint a picture of my existence.

I am a child who appreciates the struggles of my mother. I am a man who realizes his privilege and uses it to explore those who are oppressed. I am a Latino, proud of my heritage; yet, unfamiliar with it because of the ripple effect of oppression that white America threw at my grandparents, then my parents, and now at me. I am a gay man, proud of the acceptance that I have allowed of myself, proud to say this is me, proud to be whom I really am.

Remember those years of torture, those days, those moments, when with one word "fag," I would feel as small as a bug able to be smashed at any time.

Remember being a victim afraid to be you. Remember standing up for yourself. Remember standing up to an attacker and saying "No." I am proud of my many shades. I am proud of my struggles. I am proud of me.

Where I Am From

Candace Nikki Rogers

I am from many identities, which makes it hard sometimes
I am from a broken home, with one parent
I am a woman still oppressed in a male dominated world, trying to be all that I can and so much more
I am an African-American holding all the historical baggage that comes with that
I am Seminole and Cherokee, trying to find out what that really means, but not being able to find the answer
I am from a mindset of reckless endangerment to cure the woes and tribulations of life
The youngest of 4 children, but the protector of all
The Griffith wings on which so many peoples' hopes rest
I am from a land founded on "justice and freedom for all" but is so

far removed from that concept

I am from a land that could cause the rivers to run red based on
a history of injustice, death, murder, and inequality; where all my
ancestors from my many identities, have been persecuted at one
point or another and still are to this day

I am from anger, resentment, pain, hurt, tradition, culture, hate,
abuse, religion, sacrifice, love, but most of all, I am from THIS world.

Where I Am From

Julie J. Park

I am from a place where the question
"Where are you from?" can never be asked innocently because it is
always asked with an expected response of some exotic land, far far
away

So where am I from?

I am from a first grade lunch table where I was asked if it hurt to see
out of my eyes because they were so small.

I am from an Asian American immigrant dream that followed
suburban white flight to 13 years in classrooms where I was the only
different face.

I am from language school class where I was the worst at speaking
what was supposedly "my own" language.

I am from a country that doesn't know where to place my
experiences with blacks or whites, not understanding that they are
my own.

I am from a culture which tells me that rejecting my own people is
not self-hatred of my race, but simply moving up in the world.

Just like when the disappointed asker asks "no, where are you
REALLY from?" when I say in perfect, unaccented English that I was
born and raised in far exotic suburbs of Dayton, OH
I know that if I asked that question again
I could answer
I am from a family of Korean patriots who resisted Japanese
imperialism and still resists 37,000 US troops
I am from immigrant dreams to build a better life through education
From a community of celebration, of galbi and kimbap, kimchi and
boricha, strong smells and slurps
From my mother's prayers and my father's gentle love
A grandbaby of the Asian American movement—of Yellow Power,
shutting down campuses to win Ethnic Studies, and above all, the
philosophy of "serve the people."
Of love/hate relationships with always more love than hate
From the right to define myself
I am my own story
the right to say, I am from where I am
and have the last word
because I am the only one who can answer that question.

Where I Am From

Susana Hernandez

What am I? Soy una Mexicana. My parents left their native country
of Mexico to come to the U.S. for bigger and better things. But was
it really better? Their children were born in the U.S. so am I really a
Mexicana? I was raised in a society that saw me as a waste of time

and money. Now I have been accepted into a society where they see it as o.k.

That I'm a Mexicana because I'm educated, but they still see my people as invaders to their beloved U.S. So how am I Mexicana if I have never lived in the poverty stricken country where most of my family still lies? I was born in U.S. but at times I'm treated as if I had just swam across the Rio Grande. I go to Mexico and my family and friends see me as "you've become one of them." So what am I, who am I? Can I be loyal to both countries? Will either country ever accept me for who I am? Soy una Mexicana, Soy una Americana and I'll do what I can to represent both countries as well as I can. Because I am me and that's who I am.

Where I Am From

Ivania Hernandez

I am from the dreams of a single mother who cleaned houses for a living so I wouldn't have to. I am from the admiration, inspiration, determination of those who set a path for me to follow. I am Hyphenated-America where I must learn to balance and not just assume that everyone will have tolerance. I am a constant flow of thoughts that run day and night. I ponder on what I can be or what I should be...

How did I end up being me? I am the sparkle in the eyes of a 7 year-old brother who sees in me a super hero like no other. I am also the one with confusion of why my 17 year old brother believes dropping out of school is the solution.

I am from where people like me are expected to not succeed; tumble

and fall and act like money is all we need to get us out of our
"misery."
I am from where the beat of the tambour makes me sing and
occasionally yell out one of the famous Mexican gritos, Ay ay ay!
With pride I stride and every day I attempt to fly. So ahhumm...
Excuse me here I come!

Where I Am From

Karlen N. Suga

I am from a land where tradition meets the new era

Where fiery gods and snowy goddesses did battle, but in the end, no
one was victorious

It is where people of all cultures become family forever, even if they
just met a few seconds ago

Where you will never walk anywhere without receiving a warm smile

This is where people came to seek a better life—for not only
themselves, but for many generations to come.

The fields of sugarcane tell many stories here; all in different
languages, but of the same goal

This is the place where you will find adobo, tamales, mashed
potatoes, wonton, and sushi all on the same restaurant menu

Everyone is Aunty, Uncle, Bruddah, Sistah, and Cuzin—but most of all, loved and respected above everything else

Where families celebrate Chinese New Year, 4th of July, cheer on friends at the Miss Hawai'i Island Filipina Pageant, dance in a Hula Halau, watch Pow-Wows, and have fun at Bon Dances every year

This is where goodbye is never just that—it is always an invitation, a STRONG request to come visit again

I am from every culture on this planet, but most of all I am me

Aloha reigns supreme here and it is shown from the serene pastures of Waimea, the waterfalls of Akaka and Kahali'i, the clear blue waters of Kiholo, the deserts of Ka'u/Pahala, the fiery lava of Pu'u O'o, Punalu'u's rich black sand, the snowy slopes of Mauna Kea and Mauna Loa, and the rainforests of Pana'ewa

I am from love, respect, compassion, understanding, and diversity

I am from Hawai'i.

Where I Am From

Aretha M. Perry

I am from a long line of educated people—educated from the field, educated from the street, educated from life, educated from America's version of a proper institution.. . .My grandfather tilled the field that was not his own; my great, great grandmother nursed children that were not her own; my father picked cotton (believe it or not); my mother taught piano lessons to pay her way through college.

I am a product of Mississippi, Louisiana, and Missouri; I love tea cakes, hot water cornbread, and I make a mean sweet potato pie....

There is a part of me that cannot explain where I am from. I am a lost child in search of a purpose; I am a Christian, a strong believer of God, but yet I question everything that is in His play. I am a female who constantly redefines her identity; I am black; I am African-American; I am black, I am an AMERICAN, right?

Where I am from, you go to church on Sunday morning, noon and night. If you are not at Thursday night choir rehearsal, then you better be in the choir stand on Sunday. If you stay up all night on Saturday, then you better be at church the next day, cause where I am from, the Deacon's daughter better do things right.

Where I am from, you wear skirts to church and if you have on pants you are called rebellious. If you wear skirts that are too short, your dad calls you a this and your mom says you look like a that.

Where I am from, the expectations of others stress you to the point of sickness. I am confined to man's timeline, instead of God's timeline.

Where I am from will dictate where I will end up.

Where I Am From

Tiarra Netter

I come from a conspiracy. A conspiracy to hide the plain harsh truths of my family's reality. I come from Big Family gatherings where all is well, where the family matriarch is the thread of our family's fabric. I come from a home that despite the statistics is inclusive of both a mother and a father. It's funny cause it was the misleading behaviors of the two of them that have created this "Fallacy" that I call life. I come from a place called "home" that suddenly no longer existed. Despite all of the mishaps and misunderstandings I come from love. A love so strong it caused two people to endure and struggle silently so that I felt no discomfort. I came from a love so profound, sacrifice on the parts of my parents meant that I could enjoy a life of comfort and stability which are the roots to my success story. I come from strength. Strength that flows from many sources, the main one being my parents. I have learned from them to depend on inner strength that lies within me and to never let life's struggles get me down. It's this strength that has sustained me through my life's new experiences as a MOTHER. I'm from a place where my status as a single mother is seen as negative, where I am seen as the reason for the breakdown of the "traditional" family! Never mind my accomplishments, all they see is a "welfare mom." I come from stereo types and pre-conceived notions of being lazy and "uneducated." I also come from a place where a simple "I love you mommy" can melt my heart at an instant. I'm from a place that longs for my child to have a home, thus the reason for my struggle! I come from hope and determination that drives me to excel for not only me but her. I'm not from a place, but rather a life of different experiences that continue to shape me into the person I am today, a person who is not stagnant, but is continually growing!

Where I Am From

Rebecca Hossain

+ I am not from one place.

+ I am from Texas, Brazil, and France.

+ I am from Bangladesh and Puerto Rico.

+ I am from America.

+ I am from a place that stresses a singular identity; a place that always labels me a foreigner.

+ I am from the rich white suburbs all over the world.

+ I am from a place where I am taught that to be accepted I must deny the many cultures that make me, me.

+ I am from a place where the question, "Are you Saddam Hussein's daughter?" never goes without a laugh.

+ I am from a place where the values I was taught at home conflict with those of mainstream society.

✦ I am from a place where women stay at home and men are the breadwinners; a place where my dad prays five times a day and my friends compliment the "pretty rugs" that he kneels upon.

✦ I am from a place where racism thrives because putting "them" down, brings "us" up.

But...I am from a place that stresses love and happiness.

✦ I am from a family that teaches and supports me; a family that, regardless of our many identities, is incredibly unified.

✦ I am from a place where I have created my own identity.

✦ I am from the world; a place that encompasses both good and bad, and a place that forces you to pave your own path.

Where I Am From

Cynthia Payne

I am from the Bluegrass of Kentucky and horses that live across the street.

I am from a private school, pre-K through 12.

I am from assimilation even though I didn't know I was being assimilated.

I am from Latin masses, veils, holy days of obligation, and not eating meat on Friday, every Friday.

I am from not being accepted by those that look like me.

I am from "she acts like she's white."

I am from being accepted the most by the ones that I "act" like—but only accepted the most—not completely.

But, I am from love, support, discipline, dominance and privilege.

I am from the blessings of God.

On a lighter note....

I am from music.
I am from laughter.
I am from summers of baseball.

I am from silliness, craziness, and playfulness.

I am from smiles.
I am from songs.
I am from sunshine.

I am from pigtails.

I am from Wildcat basketball.
I am from Butler basketball and Cardinal baseball.

I am from confidence.
I am from frosts.
I am from residence halls and Jordan Jazz.

I am from growth.
I am from a wonderful college experience.
I am from what is to come and excited!

Who I Am...Where I Am From

Sterling Garcia

✦ I am from the city that never sleeps, where dreams become reality.

✦ I am a person who has been blessed with the opportunity to further myself, and the intelligence to take advantage of those opportunities.

✦ I am from a small apartment where I had to share a small bedroom with three others up until I left at the age of 18.

✦ I am from a broken home, where my mom had to be both father and mother, and I had to be a father figure.

✦ I am from a place where you had to carry a blade in your pocket in order to feel safe.

✦ I am a person who had to be aware of what colors to wear in order not to be killed.

✦ I am from a place where I am considered a Dominican when I am in the United States and a "gringo" when I'm in the Dominican Republic.

✦ I am from a grammar school where you had to stand up whenever the principal or pastor walked into the classroom, as a sign of respect.

✦ I am from a neighborhood where you always had to literally "watch your back" in order to not get your chain stolen off your neck.

✦ I am a person who has been loved and been in love.

✦ I am a person who has been able to see the world and be thankful for what we have as Americans.

✦ I am a person who has seen war at the age of 21.

✦ I am a role model for my two younger sisters, even though it is probably one of the hardest roles that I fill.

✦ I am old to those around me and young to the rest of the world.

I'm a man, a Veteran, an American
I'm a son
I'm a big brother
I'm a friend, an acquaintance
I'm a college student,
I'm a frat guy
I'm a leader
But in the end...I'm just me.

Where I Am From

Jose Castillo

I am from a moment in time where two kids acted on a whim.
I am from a home that was filled with contention and sorrow.
Where walking on eggshells was a much needed skill.
I am from a family of pioneers, migrant workers, and alcoholics.
I am from a people struggling to find their identity, Latino, Chicano,
    Hispanic or Pocho? (neither from here or there)

I am from a people whose fe en la Virgen is unshaken and the love of
    Dios y Jesus is richly engrained in our culture.

I am from a family torn by vices and addiction,
    a family of abuses and abused.

> *I am the older brother, the strong one who couldn't*
> *cry.*
> *I am the example.*

I am a pioneer.
I am a husband and father. Both responsibilities I hold
    sacred.
I am a Mormon.
I live in a state where 90% are of the same religion.
I am in control of my ONDA!—A toda madre o un
    desmadre!
I am a student, I am a leader, I am a follower, I am a
    survivor,
I am me!

CHAPTER 3

Celebration, Hope, Survival, Flawless, Dreams, Determined

Where I Am From

Akirah Jerelle Bradley

I am from a world of not knowing
A world of confusion and struggle
I am from a family that is not certain of their true roots that identify
as African American
I am from a galaxy of emotions
From the tears I've cried, and the obstacles I've overcome

I am from the womb of the strongest Black Woman I know, My
Mother and a direct product of an ordained deacon, My Father
A father who I love and look up to
But it is he who has disappointed me most in my lifetime
I am from hurt, pain, sorrow, but also love, joy, and serenity
I am a true "city girl," whatever that means
From the beautiful city of Brotherly Love
Where crime is high but the sense of community is higher
I am not from the block with corner stores, 25 cent hugs and $2.00
cheesesteaks
I am from where some African American sista's and brotha's think I
am not down
Or that I don't struggle because I live across from a country club
I am from being one of the first African-American families on my
block
I am from the rarely mentioned East Philly
I am from a family of Christians that does not condone same sex
relationships
I am from where I was abandoned and disowned because my sexual
orientation does not fit into mainstream society's norm
Where people get distracted by my makeup, fancy jewelry and
clothing
Judging and assuming immediately that I must be heterosexual
Well for all of those that assumed, listen to my truth now, I am NOT!
I am from where I was told I won't succeed because I am lesbian
Where my heart bleeds confronting my spirituality versus the gender
I love
More recently I am from a mother and sister who has accepted me
for who I am
Thank God

I am from a world of no regret but many mistakes
I am from where every struggle makes me stronger
I am a gift from the true heavens above
I have the ability, drive, ambition, and passion to be me
I am from where I walked some of the more difficult paths in life and
I continue to look at tomorrow as a day full of opportunities
I am truly grateful of where I am from

Where I Am From

Jessie Cordova

I am from a land from a far away place…where the drugs and the violence roam. I am from building 409, the "toughest building on the toughest block from one of the toughest neighborhoods in Brooklyn." I am also from the toughest floor in 409. Why? Because I lived next door to one of the biggest drug dealers in Brooklyn. You can say I am from a place where the drugs and violence were literally under my nose. But I am also from another place—I am from Apartment #A-3 in that building. A-3 was a whole new world for me. In A-3 there was an endless amount of love, support, friendship, advice, understanding, and care. That was my true place of origin. So while the entire world would be crumbling down outside, I was safe in A-3; my safe haven, my classroom, my home.

I come from a single-parent home and am proud and happy of it. I would not be the person that I am if it were any other way. I come from a place that taught me that you could be down but never out—a place where you looked out for yourself and each other—a place where each family member had more than one role. My mother is mom and dad. I am daughter, sister, and mother. My brother is son, brother, and father. I am from a place where you always had more on your plate than what you were really hungry for. I mean that both literally and figuratively.

Expectations of effort were always high and greatly appreciated. High expectations...high hopes. Simple, no problem.

I come from a place where in school I wasn't expected to even speak well and that was what made me want to show them. Eagle classes, SP classes, honors classes, AP classes, extracurricular activities, majors, grades, awards recognition. That is what I have done because that is what I know, what I want, what I will continue to be as I grow. Some of it I looked for and found, but most of them found me. I come from a place—my mother—that gives me the strength, the power, the motivation, and the reason to go on and on. For God, for her, for me, for my brother—I will do everything!

Where I Am From

Andrew Villanueva

I am from unstable grounds externally buildings fall, homes are destroyed some go temporarily insane some cry some leave, but some come together.

Internally people are laid off, drop out of school, go temporarily

insane, cry, leave, but some people come together.
I am from a land of constant sunshine a reminder, that no matter how shaky things may be, the land and people go on thriving.

I am from senseless black on brown violence. RIP T-shirts, racial profiling, smog, murdered friends, wounded loved ones, a virtual black tunnel with a bright light at the end for those who dare to dream past high school graduation.

I am from the center of the universe: snow, mountains, oceans, beach, cities, farms, major cities, and small suburbs are all half hour away.

I am from a group of kids playing in the street who dared to dream, and went on to feel failure and success.

Where I Am From

Kassandra Rodriguez

Marc Anthony, Si Te Vas blasting, cars honking, bustling of buses.

The aroma of arroz con pollo y platanos maduros making its way to my stomach.

The 2 train screeching into the station. The wonderful screams of children delighted by the cold water drenching them from the fire hydrant.

There are no backyards or flowerbeds here. There are projects and public parks.

Want to see Yankee Stadium hop on the 6 like J.Lo, wishing Big Pun was still on the block wearing that sound made me race down 5 flights of stairs just to get my teenage mutant ninja turtle ice cream from Mr. Frosty.

"Kassandra, ven aqui," I heard my grandma, I mean abuelita as she likes to be called, out the window.

Telefono para ti.

Wishing I could stay in Nueva York yeah.

I'm from the Bronx, I'm from Puerto Rico. Most importantly I know where I am going.

Where I Am From

Lesley-Ann Brown

Je suis de Montreal, Canada...but am I really?

I'm from a long line of proud Jamaican people; an island known for its reggae music, fried snapper, jerk chicken, and its beautiful beaches; an island who fought for its independence from England and is now choking on the vomit of its economic, political, and social deterioration because of it.

I am from a family who runs away from problems—migrating from Jamaica, to England, to Montreal, to Florida. I'm from a world where you're punished for doing the right thing, for displaying endurance and drive. I am the epitome of the saying "without struggle there can be no progress."

I am an uncertain, beat up, exhausted black girl hiding behind the mask of a strong, powerful, educated, self-empowered, and self-motivated black woman. I am not "Free at last, free at last, thank God Almighty, I'm free at last." I'm haunted by my past, struggling through the present and terrified of the future.

I am...Je ne sais pas! I don't know but I do know that...I'm trying to be a role model to underprivileged, undereducated, and overlooked youth. I'm trying to be a woman that my younger sister and my niece can look up to.

I'm trying to be a living testimony that, even though things don't always go the way that they should, if you trust in God you can be reassured that your steps are ordered by Him.

I'm trying to surpass the social obligation of each one reach one because I want to reach many. I want to love with my actions, touch with my heart, and change with my life.

I am not today...I am TOMORROW!

Where I Am From

LaTasha Smith

I am from a place of broken windows and stray gun shots. A place of grandmother's wisdom and grandfather's love. I am from a place of psst....psst...psst...bitch. I am from my mothers tears, joys and hopes, I am from a family that needs me to be something better. I am from a family that needs me to be something better. I am from a land where my people were stolen and taught nothing but expected to know everything, a land rich with resources but starving of people. A place where it was ok to steal children and kill them too. A place where the blacker you were the harder the smack. I am from Africa. I am also from a place that was claimed by another nation. A place where our land was our God. Where we prayed with every step. A land that was again stolen. A land that holds my ancient ancestors and their spirits run freely with me now. I am from a place where I won't choose. I will not choose my African ancestry without explaining my native ancestry. I live in America without embracing America. I am black, Cherokee and Choutou.

I am from a place where my young brothers need me to succeed so they will know that they can too.

Where I Am From

Briza Juarez

I am from—

+ The sounds of waves and cool sand on bare feet.

+ The love and strength of my mother.

+ A home where my father's commands were law and his fists his executioners.

+ The smell of frijoles and tortillas on the Comal.

+ The sound of my nana's voice as we sipped Café con Leche.

+ A summer lemonade stand to pay for the public neighborhood pool.

+ Drives to Mexico to visit my family.

+ The Fourth of July fireworks lighting the night sky.

+ Sweet oranges and sour lemons with salt.

+ The sounds of angry arguing at night and the comforting voice of my brother.

+ Believing in prayer and accepting what you can't change and changing what you can.

+ An alcoholic man and a woman who broke free.

+ Drama and dance classes and lights and music.

+ A latch key and making dinner for my family, while waiting for my mom and dad to come home from work.

+ Persistence to prove I could do more than others believed…Fear and overcoming it from hope and pride and endurance.

I am the first to pursue a college education.

Where I Am From

Denise Herrera

From the Sandia Mountains to the bright balloons
And the green chili casseroles to the night sky moon
From the adobe buildings to the red sunset
And places I have not met
From the children playing outside
To all the places I choose to hide
From the garden that my grandpa planted
To all the seeds I take for granted
And the family who chooses to see the best there is
in me

From the teacher who gave me hope
To the parents that gave me dreams
And all those people in-between
From the desert in the hot golden sun
This is where I am from
New Mexico.

CHAPTER 4

Bridges,
Looking Back/Looking Forward,
From Here <u>and</u> There

Where I Am From

Nicolas Los Baños

*I come from fire, from the red-hot
Power found in the union of our souls.
Mom, dad, grandparents: both sides,
Every cousin and his wife and his wife.
Staring out into the ocean, the red ocean.
Ku no ha, I au ka mokupuni o ke ahi*

Ka `āina mohala me ka wai, `ena o ka honua
Land on fire, red, royal: power.

I turn in circles to see another,
Another flame, slowly flickering
Against the goza window coverings
Lights out again, darn HELCO, or those drunk drivers!
Shoganai ne, shinpai nai de.
Ima, nani o shite iru? Wakaranai.
Yoisho, get off your butt, find more candles
Just not too many, might bring termites.

Now in flight I go, to see where I come
From feathers and blood, crumpled benjamins.
Rapid tongues masked by the eagle.
God bless America, look at who you are.
Striking out Fur Elise, and Canon in D:
Aye Jesus! Wrong note. Suman? Butbut? Same
    difference.
 Stars and stripes forever, the yellow sun, too?

A return to the moist back yard
Somersaults and twists, higher than my head
Upside down power, grace, perfection
Such talent, no spotlight, so what?
Balancing on koi pond border walls
One hand, nope, two. Back arched
Hey, I see my foot, How'd it get there?

Dismount. Ten-O or nine-point-nine-seven-five
I say 5.7, but it's all good.
Where I am from, I'm still dizzy
Wait till the head rush goes away
Then I'll tell you something more
Oh well, sun going down.
Better go inside befo, mom get mad.

Bocha or kaukau first?
No matters, but mom like us hurry.
Oh, yes! Hamburger Helper and rice
Passions orange guava in da plastic cup
Pepa plates is fine, no need wash dishes
Mo, betta li, dat, no? Yea, yea, das how.
She go ma Chinet, da bess!

Ok, bocha time den time fo, moe
Da Japanee wash clot, mo, good
'cuz make you feel mo, clean and stuff.
Yup no what? Homework? Kanji flashcards?
Nah, I goin, buss out Makaha Sons.
Dem buggas, dey make you go moemoe.
K den, I guess I jus, go sleep.

Where AM I from? You no can tell.
I can tell, but den I no can.
Too much tinking already, no can go sleep!
Bumbai all habuts in da morning
When mom come fo, wake me up.
Ahh, das ok, I get plennie time.

45

Jus, wake me up so I no miss da good cartoons

Aye, try wait, Is Friday, no?

Where I Am From

E.K. Lewis

I am me—proud, intelligent, yet lost
I am struggling with conflicts that are hard to resolve
I am loved and protected by many
I am judged and ridiculed by those who don't know me
I have been blessed by God, yet am being chased by the devil
I have confidence that one day we will all walk on clouds and not be burdened.
I am finding out more about myself from others.
I am a daughter who is incredible, smart mouthed and sassy with her father and talkative joy to her Angel mother.
I am a communicator, instigator and a regulator
I am me—I change—because you are missing. Or what is in store for you.
I slip and fall and always get back up—Success is yet to come!

Where I Am From

Jessica Barron

Where I am from is difficult to say…

I am from two separate worlds, brought together by a divine mystery.

I am from rich colors, dark secrets, hidden emotions, new beginning, and vibrant expression.

I am from sun and snow
Hope and fury
Grace and elegance
Groomed for success, designed for the struggle, made whole by the process, fearful of the progress and success of an expectant future.
Trying diligently to live up to the call in a place that doubts me and allows me to be only one or mark "other"
Black or brown
Past or present
Choose sides, make alliances, or stand-alone
Where will I fall? Where will I lie?
When it is all said and done who will He say that I am?
A daughter of strength
A sister of wisdom
A lost child with too many places to call home

I may live in separate worlds that may not meet today or tomorrow but they have made me who I am:
Ready and willing, self-conscious and awkward, unique and unconventional challenged by the challenging and hopeful for tomorrow.

I come from two separate worlds that have given me a call to unity and a chance to stand together.

Where I am from is a road map to where we are going.

Where I Am From

Adiam Tesfay

They are teenagers that put their lives on the front lines so I could grow up free and safe.

They are the ones who left all they knew and loved in order for my life to be filled with opportunity.

They are the ones who spent the last 20 years working harder than they ever have so I could live a wonderful life and be educated.

They are the ones who decided to become American citizens and lose even more of their roots so I could enjoy life.

They are me and I am them.

I am the one who translated this American language at 2 years old for parents who didn't understand it or speak it.

I am the one who taught my 7-year-old sister at 5 years old.

I am the one who raised my siblings at age 7 so my parents could work more.

I am the one who only spoke English at school Monday–Friday and learned Tigrinia and my heritage on weekends.

I am the one who left home to go to college but had no one to give me guidance and support at home.

I am the one who is struggling to be African-American

> *I am Habesha*
> *I am first generation*
> *I am determined*
> *I am woman*
> *I am daughter of God*
> *I am rich in opportunity*
> *I am American*
> *I am mother of many*
> *I have not yet begun to know me.*

Where I Am From

Katie Curiel

I am
The Highest Mountain
The Deepest Ocean
The River that runs
The Winding grass blowing with the wind
The sweet smell of the flower blossom
The juicy nectar of the ripe fruit

The sting of the bee and the sweetness of its honey.
I am a child of this earth.
A spirit of this universe.

I come from a tree
Mighty and strong
Rooted of history
Bearer of good things
Yet dependent on its environment
Fragile and vulnerable

I come from a tree
With roots long stretching from
Country to country
Continent to continent

I grow from the nurturing and calmness
Of others on my fellow earth
I feed off this and use this strength to be the shade
  for others
Protection from the storm the air to live

A history of any people and life
Past and present
A gift for tomorrow
A hope for tomorrow.

Where I Am From

Devetta Blackman

Where I am from is a question that I often ask myself a million times and with every different answer comes new challenges, ideas, goals, and values that I learned about myself. I am from a place that often times you are stuck between a rock and a hard place. That you look and act one way you are often called or told "you are acting black," just because you wear your pants below your butt. On another hand, if you talk a certain way or dress a certain way "you are acting white." I am that girl who is too educated for the "hood" and learning just enough for my peers in college. What is a girl to do when it is her against the world or "me against the world" in the world of 2 Pac?

Where I am from I learned that the code of the streets is the law and that you are bound more by that code than the law itself. That for me, while my suburban peers didn't have to worry about coming and going to school, I look out my window and see the CD's, BD's, and many other gangs. Growing up, I was determined to make it. Now I enter my last year at NIU and I look back at the "hood" and look at me now and I think where am I from.

Where I Am From

Anonymous

I am the lovechild of two individuals. Born in the motherland in the country of Nigeria. A place where people are aggressive and the weather is hot. A place with good foods like yellow rice, plantains, and looloo. I am from a land that is proud to praise the Lord. A tribe where everyone's name has a biblical meaning. I am a product of my parents who gave me the name SAFE JOURNEY TO HEAVEN. I am a survivor of New York City. I am a first cousin to over 50 people. I am a sister and a middle child with 3 sisters and a brother. I am a peacemaker, an introvert. I am a Southern girl. A lover of people, a lover of fun. I am sensitive, outgoing; energetic, cool, loving, welcoming and passionate.

I am fanatic about dance, choreography, pageants and modeling. I am easily inspired by others and cherish personal growth and development. I am from the city of Atlanta where the people are talented and interesting. A place where there are 8 lane highways and heavy pollution. I am from a university in which I've contributed in making significant transitions in student life. I am resourceful and inspiring. Romantic and thoughtful. I am from here, I am from there. I am this, I am that. I am who I am.

CHAPTER 5

Brilliant, Talented, Strong, Perseverance, and Persistence

Where I Am From

Charmaine Lastimoco

I am from lights that cause day to last 24/7
the clink of coins falling in metal bins
cards shuffling in the night
glitzy shows and smoky bars

I am from the desert, brown and open,

hot days and cool nights
dry wind and sand storms

I am also from remnants of an island country
   with the flavor of another fused into my bones
   so my skin is a yellow-brown as the
      Vendan house I remember from childhood.
   from "adobo" and "dinaguan"
      folk dances and karaoke
      thick accents and eating with my hands.

But most importantly,
   I am from the adventures and struggles
      the displacement and reinvention
      the strength and the will
      of two amazing Filipino travelers
      who came together and made me, me.

Where I Am From

Rouel Garingo Velasco

I'm from a place where love, joy and acceptance reign all over the islands. Where the Spirit of Aloha has flourished throughout the Hawaiian chain and beyond. Where the shaka hand signs, wet juicy kisses on the cheeks and warm friendly hugs are commonly found among the island people. Where the sunset reflects the beauty of the land as well as its diversified inhabitants. Where the cool blue ocean waves pound the shores, speaking to the heart, telling myself to be calm and patient. Where the cool breezy winds are guiding my journey in life making sure I get there safe and sound. Where strangers become your best friends. Where everyone has one love and one heart. I'm from a place where everyone is Ohana or family. Where no one gets left behind or forgotten.

I am from a community that has a history for bad reputation. Where drugs, violence, and teen pregnancies have plagued the streets. Where its people have endured isolation and rejection from people outside of the community. It is that kind of stigma which keeps the people away from pursuing their lifelong dreams and ambitions. Where school children are learning, not knowing they are immune to the distinct smell of the chicken farms that is located a couple of houses away from the school. Where disputes are usually solved with the closed fist. Having an actual audience watching rather than stopping the fight. Where respect is gained by winning fights rather than winning high grades. I am from a community that is not only HOT in climate, but also in temper.

Still, I am from a community where positive changes are taking place. I'm from a community where the tides are gradually rising and the winds are slowly shifting. Where hope, encouragement and confidence bring new life to the community. Where old friends are reuniting, enemies are becoming friends; neighbors are lending a helping hand, and a community striving for the betterment of its people. Where the people are coming together to fight the drugs and violence out for a better, safe and clean community. Where football, Homecoming Week and other community celebrations has always been the driving forces that keeps the community together. Where students of today's generation are making big differences not only for themselves but also for the community. I am from a community of perseverance and resiliency.

I'm from a family of two parents and 4 brothers. Where my parents are first-generation immigrants from the Philippines. Where the Filipino culture is deeply rooted in our hearts, minds, language, and food. Where my parents are strict in their manner making it really difficult to tell whether they are showing their love and affection or just preventing me from having fun. Also, whose parents will declare the kind of work I will have, the person whom I will marry and the place I will reside. I'm from a home where constant arguing took place. Where no one could understand each other's reasoning or justification. Where brotherly love was not always so brotherly. Where a visible line distinguishes myself from my brothers. Distinguishing myself for having different views, preferences, and interests. Through it all, I am from a family where God, our Father, has been keeping us tightly bonded together.

I am from a family where the Christian Faith is the foundation of our living. Where we believe that in all things, whether it is good or bad, to give thanks to the Almighty Lord. We also believe that we can go through any obstacles or trials with the help of Christ. Just ask and it will be given to you, seek and you will find, knock and the door will be opened to you. I'm from a family where we live by faith and not by sight. Where we all go to church together and grow together. I am from a family that is strongly bonded and guided by the grace of the Almighty God.

This is where I am from.
I am from Hawaii.

I am from Ma'ili of Wai'anae.
I am unique.
I am a Christian.
I am a Filipino-American.
I am Rouel Garingo Velasco.

Where I Am From

Cameron J. Harris

I am from undefeated attitudes and the ability to persevere through difficulties. I am from Sunday dinners. As I emerge from unforgotten dreams, I am made aware of the necessity to be determined. I am from the negative stereotype that has been placed upon black males. I am from a divergent world of those who haven't gone anywhere and those who forget where they have come. I am strengthened by a difficult past and uplifted by a promising future while embracing every opportunity the present presents me. I am defined not by my experience but by my reactions to these events. I am whatever I choose to be.

Where I Am From

Randall P. Bogard

I am a young man that sits in front of you. From the land of the Jackson's and the Steel Mill. Where for me following the rules was expected. Knowing that getting into the wrong things could have me six feet deep. Where being the best and doing good was all I could think about. For knowing that my aspirations would take me as far as long as family and friends were around. To considering school and sports a job and a passion. To believing that the only one that could stop me is the man upstairs and myself. Seeing that getting out means you are stronger. Being a role model is a privilege: This also means failing is not an option, but struggle and triumph is part the journey. To say that I am a grown man would not be fair to the words. To say that I am one that works everyday to be better is. Those that look at me believe that life is great and easy for me. But those that get to know me understand who I am and love me for that.

Where I Am From

Anonymous

Where I come from, I was the over-protected one.
I was teased for who I was.
It wasn't okay for a nine-year-old to have
a teenage pregnant sister.
Moreover, I was not allowed to be told of her reality.
What were these family meetings that I could not go
    to?
When the baby came, I began to realize where I
    came from.

Where I am from, I can title my identity but not
    experience my lifestyle.

It was no longer okay to be a kid anymore,
I had to be the savior.
My brother quit college and joined the military.
There was a new expectation for me to be the
    college graduate.

Where I'm from, I needed to leave.
Loneliness, confusion, fear, and obligated happiness
    were
amongst the many emotions I experienced.
I did move away for college.
The pressure to be at home was too much.

Where I am from, the people began to look at me as
    rebellious.
It took five years of college to find my voice.
Dare I say it? Yes, I am gay!

A place that talked about diversity, could not include
    this culture.
The place where I came from, remains a distant
    place.

Where I am from, I was taught to respect other
    cultures.
It was built into the Filipino culture not to talk unless
    spoken to.
This is contradiction in itself, but I try to respect it.
I may have offered an unwanted statement
but I struggle to live out my identity.

I know there is understanding and support for me.
I just wish it grew in the place
Where I Am From.

CHAPTER 6

Freedom and Running To, Not From

Where I Am From

Sarah M. Childs

Look at my family...that is how you know where I am from.
I am from hot apple pie, mole, and dim sum.
I am from a broken family, with the most beautiful and strong
woman to call mom and a father who is living in his own world.
I am from an interracial couple where my Mexican roots dominated
and where I get the appreciation for my Chinese blood when I see

the handsome face of my grandpa and all his brilliance.
Where "De Colores" was a favorite song sung as a child with my
Mexican grandma and then there was Patsy Cline and Jim Reeves
with grandma and grandpa Childs.
Then there is Aaron, my older brother. We are from a childhood of
playing She-Ra and He-Man in Aaron's two-toned underwear and in
the front yard.
We are from a country that tries to promote democracy and freedom
of choice, yet when the time comes Aaron will not be able to marry
the man that he loves.
I am from a place that bitches and moans about how all the illegals
are taking American jobs but would you clean filthy toilets and floors
and break your back to make minimum wage?
I am from a place that values education yet makes accessibility to
one an increasing challenge.
I am from a place that values material possessions and money—
where the wealthiest of the wealthy could support 10 of the poorest
countries in the world and still we have starving nations.
I am from the school of thought that "si se puede!"
I am from a place with a very complex history…but I would not have
it any other way.

Where I Am From

Louna Mona

I am Hmong And Hmong means free.
I have no country.
My parents have no country.

We do not know where we are from.
In books, historians say that we are from the south of
China.
We are not Chinese, we are Hmong.
We were called Barbarians, We had to assimilate or
die.
Therefore, we fled and found another land.

This land is beautiful, peaceful and nurturing.
This land is on the mountaintops of Laos, far from
civilization.
25 years ago we were taken from this land to come
to America.
Where is America?
America is far, far away, above the clouds.
Why did we come to this strange land?
Hmong people fought in a secret war, assisted to US
CIA in the Vietnam war.

I am a first generation Hmong woman, Caught in
two worlds,
that sometimes collide.
At home, I am obedient and quiet.
Outside, I am independent, outspoken and friendly.
Inside, I am strong, resilient and happy.

I am Hmong, and I am free.

Where I Am From

Anonymous

A place where my cousins, older and younger, see me. I am from a place where men objectify me, women disrespect me people talk about me, people ignore me. I am from a place where people who look like me are assumed ugly and unattractive. I am from a place where these things have been embedded to the point where I am unattractive to myself. I am also from a place to understand that things don't happen by chance but by will, not mine. I am from a place where ham and macaroni and cheese was the only meal for the week. Where you could only eat what was cheap. A place where eating healthy is a luxury. Buying clothes and shoes at the mall a rarity. A place where going outside and making mud puddles was the only recreation. I am the pride of my family and a product of my past. My future seems different than others but I accept it willingly. I am from a place where I will be myself no matter what. I am from me.

Where I Am From

Anonymous

Where I am from, contradiction blessed the ground.

Where I am from, diversity is defined in the context of cultures. There were many Asian-Americans present.

My family was one of the few Filipino-American families active with the Church.
We were the token Filipino family.
My father, the retired navy man, now a leader in the community.
My brother, the "Manoy," held his title of being the eldest very dear.
Mom, took the matriarchal role very strictly.
Lastly, there was my older sister, my "Manang," and of course, myself.
She was, and now I am, the black sheep of the family.

Where I am from, I had to represent well.
My mom was very strict in our presentation.
Was the world really looking deeply at us?
When the weekend came, I knew the house was getting cleaned.
There she was following right behind with her white glove.
My clothes needed to be kept clean for church just as well.

I had to be the perfect child.

Where I am from, my family valued our rich Filipino traditions.
I tried hard to be inclusive of all cultures.
Why did other Filipinos question my Filipino-ness?
A coconut? No! I'm just learning and appreciating
other cultures, while living my own.
So what if I could not speak Tagalog!
My parents came from the South, they spoke Visaya.

Where I grew up, expectations were prevalent and standards were high.
Yes, I received "free lunch tickets" at school.

I'm sorry I got B's with my A's.
Manoy just got C's.
English as a Second Language
I may understand Visaya, but I only spoke English.
Why was I removed from the high reading group and
 into this ESL class?

PART II

Rethinking Student Affairs

Where I Am From

Susan E. Borrego

I am from the smells of White Shoulders perfume and stale beer and
the sweet lilacs blowing in my window in the spring.
From days in the dark, smoky bars my mother worked.
I am from scary nights in empty houses, children too young to be
left alone. From "Susan, watch those boys, make sure you fix them
dinner and remember, there is laundry…"
I am from teenagers too young to parent.

I am from Vernors Ginger ale, red Kool-Aid, and empty pop bottles
exchanged for penny candy. From the "uptown" poor block, playing
outside till dark in gravel lots with broken and borrowed sports
equipment.
From no one calling me home to dinner.

I am from "Ma," the grandma who continued to raise me long after
I no longer lived with her.
From her voice and smoky laugh that lives in my center a decade
after she is gone.
I am from nights of watching the thunder and lightning outside
Ma's windows, clapping at each strike, instead of being afraid.

I am from that tough talking, tough loving grandma, straight pins
and cigarettes hanging from the corner of her mouth as she sewed.

From her cake decorating in a one-butt kitchen, making frosting
flowers on my hand and answering every question I asked.

I am from odd jobs, 4 a.m. paper routes, shoveling snow, picking
nightcrawlers and shining shoes at 6.
From Motown—"Ain't No Mountain High Enough, Ain't No Valley
Low Enough," and Aretha's "Respect" blasting right through me.
I am the "love child" never meant to be.

I am from a life-time of living in other people's homes and Ma
reminding me in whatever family crisis that the world was full of
"good people."
From other people's mothers and lightning bugs—Downriver poor
but always enough to share.
I am from hard-livin' surviving and grateful.

Where I Am From

Kathleen Manning

I'm from the place that Bruce Springsteen sings about—boardwalks, strong smells, traffic, miles of concrete…As a friend once commented, "You can take the girl out of New Jersey, but you can't take New Jersey out of the girl." I grew up on three acres of land, a big house surrounded by trees, old farms, and the Garden State Parkway. Highways, oil refineries, and diners. Anyone from New Jersey knows how to find a good diner.

I work in a place that people like me were never meant to be: working class, first-generation college student, average grades. Me, be a faculty member? Who would have thought? Despite my success (teaching award, pillar of the profession, "I've heard good things about you…"), I always feel a bit out of place. That's okay though. We need to claim our place in these ivory towers—they need our vigor, enthusiasm, and toughness.

I'm one of five children—the middle child. Older and younger siblings pivoted around me. I thought of myself as the stable one—the one who avoided alcoholism, depression, and marginal employment. Five of us—no children. We are a strange bunch. I use the plural when I talk about my childhood: "we" used to sleigh ride in the backyard, "we" used to take vacations down the shore, "we" had this great apple tree and sand pile to play in. "We" are alone now—Mom died in 1991, Dad in 2003. The house is sold now—no more trips to New Jersey—it's a blessing.

I'm not from this place, New England, but it occupies a large space in my psyche. A six year stint in Boston and 18 years in Vermont mean that I've lived most of my adult life in this odd part of the world. I can never say I'm "from" here, but I can say that I "belong" here. The beauty, the quiet, the people—they all suit me.

CHAPTER 7

Narratives, Theory,
and Student Affairs Practice

T he Minority Undergraduate Fellows Program (MUFP)
fellows have strong, rich experiences that fly in the face
of the "deficit model" of many multi-cultural theories.
The narratives declare what needs to be said about the experiences of these students in ways that theory does not. Traditional
theories on cultural pluralism and diversity in student affairs
fall short of what the fellows express. The theories, particularly
those with stage-oriented assumptions, are often irrelevant, out
of order, or misinterpreted. Racial identity development theory

does not capture what the narratives articulate. With permission from the fellows, we compiled these narratives to build a philosophy of practice based on experience rather than a philosophy of practice based on theory. They provide a window into the genuine experiences of the MUFP fellows who wrote them.

A RENEWED TYPE OF HOLISTIC STUDENT DEVELOPMENT

This work embodies and challenges the commitment of student affairs educators to address the needs of the whole student. *The Student Personnel Point of View* in 1937 and 1949 (American Council on Education, 1937, 1949); *Learning Reconsidered* (Keeling, 2004); and the best of the developmental theory on which our practice is based all refer to "wholeness" and "making meaning" (Kegan, 1982). The "Where I Am From" narratives are examples of students making meaning of their experiences. What began as an exercise became something much larger—an opportunity to create meaning and build theory to guide practice in the field.

This book and the "Where I Am From" exercise on which it is built demonstrate students' hunger to make meaning. They were asked a simple question: "Where are you from?" They eagerly stepped up to reveal what was just below the surface. This eagerness can remind student affairs educators that our pedagogy, based on students, is essential. That pedagogy, grounded in the experiences of students, can open up spaces for deeper, richer engagement. Any pedagogy—student-experience-based or abstract and non-experiential—used carelessly can shut spaces and students down. The content and practice of a pedagogy is just as important as its origin. In other words, student affairs educators must understand the influence of our pedagogy and our individual selves on students. In this book, we are attempting to bridge the gap between the pedagogy we espouse and the practice we enact.

We, Susan Borrego and Kathleen Manning, are two White women, living with the privileges that being White provides. We are not trying to define these students' lives. The narratives speak for themselves about their lives, their dreams, and the experiences they count as meaningful. But, as educators who work with students of color, we acknowledge the reality that student affairs professionals cannot avoid defining aspects of students' lives. If we are honest with ourselves, we come to understand that we use theory, our experiences as racial beings, and our understandings as educators to make judgments about students. In this book, we challenge assumptions, create a place for the expression of soul and context, and link ideas about theory and practice to a holistic expression of how students talk about themselves. The book and the narratives attempt to open a window into the genuine experiences of these students of color.

How professionals, including student affairs professionals, think about or use theory depends on their point of view. The lens of the person doing the viewing determines what is seen, and it can hide as much as it reveals. Theory can be interpreted as a model, to be played with, adapted, and changed when more knowledge or experience makes it obsolete. Or, from a one-dimensional or absolute approach, it can be seen as rigid and inflexible. From this perspective, theory becomes the enemy rather than simply a tool to aid understanding. Theory was never written to be wholly congruent with individuals or groups; it does not fit real life in a predictable or perfect way. But it can be a guide and a source of insight. Theory is meant to explain and aid understanding. But, theory can be misused when someone has an experience but misses the full range of possible meanings. These narratives provide an opportunity to expose that meaning.

THE THEORY OF THE NARRATIVES

In the grounded theory tradition of qualitative research (Lincoln & Guba, 1985), the themes we discuss emerged from the narratives. The theory we describe in the following chapters is grounded in the fellows' experiences. As authors seeking to discuss the fellows' themes and apply them to student affairs theory and practice, we did not start with theory and move to the narratives; we started with the narratives and moved to theory. The challenge for us was to stay out of the way of the narratives, which expressed the real situation much more completely than our grounded theory. This struggle is experienced by anyone who takes students' voices seriously.

I am from a long line of educated people—
educated from the field, educated from the street,
educated from life, educated
from America's version of a proper institution.
—Aretha Perry

Theory, by its nature, privileges some voices (e.g., faculty) over others (e.g., students). The voices expressed in the "Where I Am From" narratives relate understandings that may not be expressed—or may be inadequately expressed—in the "official" version of theory. This does not mean those voices do not exist or are not authentic. It means that they are not privileged in an official way. Many of the ideas expressed in the narratives occupy a different place than those that define and guide student affairs practice. Their absence in the mainstream literature reveals an urgent need for these experiences to be incorporated into and redefine student affairs theory and pedagogy. A goal of this book is to include the meaning into theory and practice without pigeonholing or stereotyping the fellows or their experiences.

SWITCHING THE QUESTIONS

These voices—similar to those expressed in women's, queer, and ethnic studies—can change the questions asked by student affairs educators. When more voices are included and different questions are asked, practice changes. When students like the MUFP fellows—students of color; students with disabilities; students who are lesbian, gay, bisexual, or transgender—are present and listened to, they change the questions asked in higher education. They challenge assumptions about inclusion and fairness, and change what is privileged as knowledge. They open the door to create new theory. This book enacts that change by privileging the narratives in the same way that conventional theory is privileged. With that refocused perspective, the construction of knowledge shifts.

Because the narratives were written from the heart, they contain a poetry and beauty not often portrayed in theory. In summarizing the themes, we have attempted to reflect the beauty of the poetry in the expression of the theory. We also hope to provoke student affairs theorists and practitioners to reflect the reality of the narratives in their theory and practice. We hope our writing decreases the space between theory and the real. While theory is informed by the everyday experience of people, it is often privileged as more authentic and meaningful than experience. If it is presented in a stripped-down version, theory can be divorced from reality. The narratives retain the essence of reality; we hope the grounded theory in these chapters does the same.

I am from two separate worlds,
brought together in a divine mystery.
—Jessica Barron

THE DIFFICULTY AND PROMISE OF CHALLENGE AND SUPPORT

Difficulty and promise coupled with challenge and support are major themes in the narratives. While student affairs professionals talk about these themes in a daily, almost matter of fact, manner, the students describe their challenges or difficulties as part of their successes. The fact that the students have persevered or are persevering might tempt us to trivialize the agonizing aspects of the experience: "Hey, they're making it, aren't they? What's the problem?"

The concept of challenge and support has been foundational in the student affairs field since the 1960s. Nevitt Sanford (1962) introduced it, and it has been extended by many others (e.g., Arthur Chickering and Erik Erikson). But while profession-

als have effectively used challenge as a form of team building or
staff development, we sometimes miss the fact that our students
have actually lived with challenge, moved through it, and continue to experience it. The fellows bring a wide range of skills to
campus born of the challenges they have experienced. The narratives help us see that challenge is present in their lives, period.
They have something to share with others (including student
affairs educators) as a result of their all-too-familiar relationship
with challenge. As authors, we have tried to avoid the tempta-
tion to romanticize their challenge as simply a character-building
experience.

USING CHALLENGE AND SUPPORT IN PRACTICE

Student affairs professionals often discuss how much challenge and how much support to build into student programs,
and some of us may become overly enamored with introducing
challenge into students' lives. Programs, services, policies, and
"environmental press" are used to encourage students to grow
and develop. Challenge is indeed a learning and group development tool, but the lives of students of color, especially those
on predominantly White campuses, may already be filled with
challenge. We may need to rethink our assumptions about building additional challenge into their already challenge-filled lives.
As the narratives demonstrate, the fellows have already lived
through a host of challenges, many of which are ongoing and
may even be compounded throughout the college years.

The questions for student affairs educators working with
students of color are, "How do we challenge students who have
faced more or different kinds of adversity than what is offered

on a college campus?" and "How do we reduce the adversity felt through racism, classism, and other 'isms' to challenge students across the whole of their identities?" To understand that wholeness, student affairs educators must understand something about the identities of students of color.

IDENTITY

Because the narratives are so personal, we must talk about identity. The current student affairs literature includes racial identity development theory that is deeper and more richly explanatory than in the past. The early racial identity development theory started from a "disadvantaged" perspective. Cross's theories (1971, 1978, 1985, 1991) of African American racial identity development, though revolutionary at the time, placed the pivot foot in pre-encounter—the stage during which African Americans identify with White culture and reject or deny membership in Black culture. While we would not deny that pre-encounter still occurs in racial identity development, the older theory does not explain racial identity development originating from a place of pride and self-respect.

Rather than starting with the dominant culture perspective as the norm, scholars of color such as Vasti Torres and Mary Howard-Hamilton (Torres, Howard-Hamilton, & Cooper, 2003); Raechele Pope (1998; Pope, Reynolds, & Mueller, 2004); Michael Cuyjet (1997; 2006); and Shaun R. Harper (2005; 2006; Harper, Byars, & Jelke, 2005; Harper, Carini, Bridges, & Hayek, 2004; Harper, Harris, & Mmeje, 2005), among others, construct theory from a self-valuing perspective. These scholars of color do not start from a perspective of disadvantage or "other dominance." They start from pride and self-respect, as described in the narratives. In their writing, the history and traditions of people of color are not lumped together as if the unique elements of self and community do not affect one's identity. Rather, the racial identity development theories of Asian Americans, African Americans, Native Americans, and Latino/as are described in respectful, contextual, and distinctive ways.

With the introduction of theory written from the perspectives of people of color, the literature is changing. Ideas about comparing better or worse, constructing a generalized norm, and inventing a unified idea of student or racial identity development are abandoned. These newer theorists, with no disrespect to the giants who went before them, are changing the way knowledge is constructed in student affairs.

Past and present theories show us that identity development for students of color is vastly different from White student development. Over the past 20 years, theorists have taken care to account for and understand cultural differences, as well as the collective experiences of oppression and marginalization. Because the early stage-like developmental theories fit too few students in meaningful ways, we acknowledge the difficulty and mistake of putting any students, particularly students of color, in stage-like boxes of development. Their experiences are too rich, diverse, and remarkable to be limited by the restrictions of those à priori stages and steps.

In the following chapters, we attempt to join the conversation articulated by the theorists of color. The narratives augment the racial identity development and multi-culturalism theories by conveying the strengths and weaknesses possessed by these students, the complexity and wholeness of identity development, and how theory can be informed and extended to encompass more fully the issues expressed in the narratives.

Like the theories developed by scholars of color, the narratives were written by persons with firsthand knowledge of race, identity, and the obstacles of oppression. Themes of pain, joy, triumph, and struggle live right on or under the surface of their words. The immediacy and ready exposure of the themes show that they were not forgotten on the journey to and through college. A simple request to write such a narrative in a place of safety and trust exposed them.

So What, Now What? Implications for Practice

Theory evolves over time. As student affairs educators who are professionals, we can use the newer identity development theory to better inform our practice. Reading groups, conference presentations, and professional development events can be catalysts for learning the newer theories. However, putting these theories into practice demands a shift in perspective. As discussed in later chapters and described in the narratives, racism and oppression are factors not to be ignored. Racial identity development without an analysis of oppression will certainly result in misinformed practice.

Student affairs educators can follow the lead of the MUFP fellows and write a "Where I Am From" narrative. How do generational differences influence your understanding of identity and development? How is the place where you are from different from or the same as where the MUFP fellows are from? Where are you from?

REFERENCES

American Council on Education. (1937). *The student personnel point of view.* Washington, DC: Author.

American Council on Education. (1949). *The student personnel point of view.* Washington, DC: Author.

Cross, W. E. (1971). The Negro-to-Black conversion experience: Toward a psychology of Black liberation. *Black World, 20*(9), 13–27.

Cross, W. E. (1978). Models of psychological nigrescence: A literature review. *Journal of Black Psychology. 5*(1), 13–31.

Cross, W. E. (1985). Black identity: Rediscovering the distinction between personal identity and reference group orientation. In M. Spencer, G. Brookins, & W. Allen (Eds.), *Beginnings: The social and affective development of Black children* (pp. 144–171). Hillsdale, NJ: Erlbaum.

Cross, W. (1991). *Shades of black: Diversity in African-American identity.* Philadelphia: Temple University Press.

Cuyjet, M. (Ed.). (1997). *Helping African American men succeed in college.* New Directions for Student Services, No. 80. San Francisco: Jossey-Bass.

Cuyjet, M. (Ed.). (2006). *African American men in college.* San Francisco: Jossey-Bass.

Harper, S. (2006). Enhancing African American male student outcomes through leadership and active involvement. In M. Cuyjet (Ed.), *African American men in college* (pp. 68–94). San Francisco: Jossey-Bass.

Harper, S. R. (2005). Leading the way: Inside the experiences of high-achieving African American male students. *About Campus, 10*(1), 8–15.

Harper, S. R., Harris III, F., & Mmeje, K. C. (2005). A theoretical model to explain the overrepresentation of college men among campus judicial offenders: Implications for campus administrators. *NASPA Journal, 42*(4), 565–588.

Harper, S. R., Byars, L. F., & Jelke, T. B. (2005). How membership affects college adjustment and African American undergraduate student outcomes. In T. L. Brown, G. S. Parks, & C. M. Phillips (Eds.), *African American fraternities and sororities: The legacy and the vision* (pp. 393–416). Lexington, KY: University Press of Kentucky.

Harper, S. R., Carini, R. M, Bridges, B. K., & Hayek, J. (2004). Gender differences in student engagement among African American undergraduates at historically Black colleges and universities. *Journal of College Student Development, 45*(3), 271–284.

Keeling, R. P. (Ed.). (2004). *Learning reconsidered: A campus-wide focus on the student experience.* Washington, DC: National Association of Student Personnel Administrators and American College Personnel Association.

Kegan, R. (1982). *The evolving self: Problem and process in human development.* Cambridge, MA: Harvard University Press.

Lincoln, Y., & Guba, E. (1985). *Naturalistic inquiry.* Beverly Hills, CA: Sage.

Pope, R. L. (1998). The relationship between psychosocial development and racial identity of college students of color. *Journal of College Student Development, 41,* 302–312.

Pope, R. L., Reynolds, A. L., & Mueller, J. A. (2004). *Multicultural competence in student affairs.* San Francisco: Jossey-Bass.

Sanford, N. (1962). *The American college: A psychological and social interpretation of the higher learning.* New York: John Wiley & Sons.

Torres, V., Howard-Hamilton, M., & Cooper, D. L. (2003). Identity development of diverse populations: Implications for teaching and administration in higher education. *ASHE-ERIC Higher Education Report, 29*(6). San Francisco: Jossey-Bass.

CHAPTER 8

The Smells and Tastes of Home

Collard greens, baked macaroni and cheese,
smothered pork chops or chicken,
homemade cornbread (not jiffy),
southern style biscuits (not pilsbury)…
–Davida S. Smith

The "Where I Am From" narratives impart a palatable sense of place, characterized by the smells and tastes of home. These smells and tastes make up the traditions of their cultures; the places they are from and will not reject. Many of the fellows refer to and use the language of their cultures in ways that twist and turn college conventions. College is the place they left home for…a place they can never really call "home." Its smells and tastes are different than those of home.

Taking the train to my grandfather's restaurant,
getting food for me and my grandmother
like arroz y gondules, white rice with caldito,
pollo guisado, pemil, and of course
bread with butter.
–Kimberly Herrera

The descriptions of the smells and tastes of home, present in so many of the narratives, are visceral and centering. The many times home is evoked points to its importance to the fellows. Student affairs educators, particularly with regard to students of color, can underestimate the importance of home and the differences between home and college. For years, higher education support programs have encouraged students to loosen their connection to home. Student affairs theory commonly supports the belief that staying too connected will decrease students' chances of succeeding in college. However, in the fellows' narratives, these connections to home are part of what sustains them. The sights and sounds of home described in the narratives are like mortar; cement that holds everything together.

The descriptions of their homes are immediate; they bring you right to that place. It is easy to appreciate the experiences and backgrounds of these students. The accounts invite you to learn something about a culture you may know nothing about. The narratives offer a glimpse into sacred parts of the fellows' lives. This is a gift these students have given us.

I am also from remnants of an island country
with the flavor of another fused into my bones
so my skin is a yellow-brown as the
Vendan house I remember from childhood.
from "adobo" and "dinaguan"
folk dances and karaoke
thick accents and eating with my hands.
–Charmaine Lastimoco

In student affairs, professionals talk about exposure to diversity and the importance of interacting with "diverse others." But do we fail to realize the potential that exists when people simply share who they are by describing the smells and tastes of home? When students share these experiences with us, they invite us into their lives. Their descriptions tell us who they are; as we read them, we're drawn into their experiences.

The narratives demonstrate how vivid and poetic people can be when they speak from experiences they know well. The narratives can remind student affairs educators of the poetry that surrounds us each day, the poetry in the lives of the students with whom we work and live. The unintentional poetry of the narratives is the rich descriptions of home; simultaneously deep and simple. They are expressions of what is important to the fellows and what parts of home they miss while in college. Every student misses some part of home, but the students of color who wrote these narratives express an acute sense of distance between the place they are from and the place they are now.

*Where I am from the most important seasonings
used in food are Adobo and Sazon. My friends laugh
at me because I put those two specific seasonings in
everything I make from rice & beans to spaghetti.*
–Kimberly Herrera

When the fellows describe grandmother's cooking, the sounds of traffic, and the colors and feelings of home, it is obvious that the sounds and tastes of home are vastly different from those on a college or university campus. College may be the place where they are nurturing and developing their hopes for the future but it is vastly different from the places they are from.

After reading the narratives, student affairs educators might question the assumptions on which we build our work. Whose perspective is represented in the art and architecture of the campus? Whose art is depicted on the walls of administrative buildings and dining halls? Whose home does your office look like? Whose traditions are represented in the library books and textbooks? How can we challenge ourselves to be more inclusive, so that the smells and tastes of college feel more homelike to these students? How do we support their navigation of both worlds?

STRENGTH THAT EMERGES FROM THE LOVE OF OTHERS

Love and caring emerge from the descriptions about the smells and tastes of home. Many of the narratives describe loving and being loved as vital elements of a fellow's strength and perseverance. They are full of descriptions about love that transforms them—love from parents, grandparents, siblings, community. Infused in these expressions of love is a legacy of something larger than a fellow's immediate family. The fellows describe people loving them unconditionally to the point where these family members endow them with dreams. The dreams of parents, grandparents, siblings, and community members (e.g., getting an education, being financially secure) have been transferred into the students' lives.

> *I came from a love so profound,*
> *sacrifice on the parts of my parents*
> *meant that I could enjoy a life*
> *of comfort and stability which are*
> *the roots to my success story.*
> *—Tiarra Netter*

In their narratives, the fellows describe the responsibility they feel to fulfill those familial or communal dreams, even if the aspiration was not initially their own. The boundary between the fellows' dreams and the others' dreams is blurred. The fellows do not describe these expectations as burdens or obligations but as contributing to their strength and sustenance. Many fellows say they are the embodiment of hope for their families and communities; they state clearly that they will not let those people down.

> *I am from the admiration, inspiration, determination*
> *of those who set a path for me to follow.*
> *—Ivania Hernandez*

Love for Others Builds Character

In addition to the love and dreams that many fellows describe as flowing toward them, some also tell how their own acts of love transform them. The act of being simultaneously inspired by someone's love while loving back inspires even more. They talk about their obligations and about the joy and sustenance they find in loving and being loved. As they serve as role models for others, bring others along from their families or communities, and generally give back to those families and communities, their resolve grows to fulfill the personal and collective dreams. They are inspired to succeed, even at this unfamiliar place called college—a place that is often unreceptive to their ways of being.

> *I am the sparkle in the eyes of a*
> *7-year-old brother who sees in me*
> *a superhero like no other.*
> *–Ivania Hernandez*

Many fellows write from the knowledge that their strength comes from people, especially younger siblings who look up to them. Repeatedly, the narratives express the idea that the fellows' must give back, that their gifts belong to a larger community than just themselves. These fellows accept a mandate to develop and use the gifts they have been given, so they can give back. They feel obligated to use the opportunities granted to them through the sacrifice of others to create something larger than themselves.

I'm trying to surpass the social obligation
of "each one reach one" because
I want to reach many.
I want to love with my actions, touch with my heart,
and change with my life.
–Lesley-Ann Brown

The challenge, the love, and the dream to create something larger than themselves is often couched in the language
of strength; strength from their families and communities, and
from within themselves. Many times, this strength is gained
through adversity.

THE STRENGTH-BUILDING POWER OF ADVERSITY

The descriptions of adversity in the narratives leave the
reader feeling that, in the experiences of these students, adversity and strength are different sides of the same coin. Complex
and contradictory statements regarding adversity, immediate,
sophisticated, and intense, abound in the narratives. Through
their poignant descriptions of broken family relationships, alcoholism, teenage pregnancies, and difficult home circumstances,
the fellows lament the pain yet communicate their triumph over
these circumstances. They contrast their success with the pain of
siblings or friends who did not make it. They list the hazards of
the street and describe the opportunities and achievements they
now celebrate.

I am from a world of no regret but many mistakes
I am from where every struggle makes me stronger
I am a gift from the true heavens above
I have the ability, drive, ambition,
and passion to be me.
–Akirah Jerelle Bradley

The wisdom expressed in the narratives is often well beyond the chronological age of the writers and not accounted for in commonly used student development models. The narrow samples on which student development theories were built included few experiences of untimely deaths of friends and classmates, little pain of poverty, and few cases of succeeding despite the odds. While few purposely seek adversity, individuals are certainly strengthened by it. The Minority Undergraduate Fellows Program (MUFP) fellows' descriptions about their experiences with adversity is knowledge that many other students can only imagine.

NOT EITHER/OR, BUT *BOTH/AND*

As described above, adversity and strength in the lives of MUFP fellows were different sides of the same coin. The lives of these students have not been filled with adversity *or* strength, but adversity *and* strength. Their focus in the narratives is not on pain in the absence of happiness. They show an amazing resilience, a remarkable ability to rise above the challenge, even when they lack support. Just as many cannot imagine the challenge of their circumstances, the love, dreams, and courage of families and friends—and of themselves—that sustains them is equally incredible. Their strength is born from deep love and sacrifice that transcends adversity. Their source of strength was in the adversity. Beyond the two-sided coin of adversity/strength, the fellows' essays brim with other expressions of the *"both/and"* of their lives. Struggle *and* love. Pain *and* happiness. Disappointment *and* triumph. Challenge *and* support. Their lives, and perhaps the lives of most students, are much more complex than simple either/or dichotomies.

> *From a place where love is a fantasy*
> *but also a safety net…*
> *–Natalie M. Byrdsong*

The *both/and* realities of challenge and support are evident in their difficult personal and home circumstances which, in many cases, are simultaneously marked by deep family love or enduring ties.

The paths that brought the fellows to higher education often are contextualized by experts as disadvantage. But, that is not what the fellows say in the narratives. In the narratives, few fellows dwell on the challenges, disappointments, and resistance they encounter each day. Rather, they describe the strength born of their particular path and how both disappointment and love nurture their goals and aspirations. They epitomize the saying, "What doesn't kill you makes you stronger."

> *I'm from the joy that filled me when coming here*
> *gave me a chance to get to know an absent dad. I'm*

95

*from the bond we discovered between us and the
struggle it took to get there.*
–Joseph "Piko" Ewoodzie

Growth in the Midst of Crisis

Student development theory informs us that growth happens in the mess, chaos, and crises of life. More than a few of these students have experienced tough lives and have persevered to attend college and earn their degrees. Some of them plan to return to their home communities, if so desired. If it is true that development occurs in crisis, these students may be the *most* developed and the *most* advanced of all.

Student development theory also claims that nothing happens without resistance. The resilience of the MUFP fellows clearly comes from that place of resistance. But, sadly, there are few places on campus that respect their responses to this resistance. Rather than recognizing their anger as an appropriate response to unjust circumstances or their mistrust as an appropriate response to broken promises, others see these responses as hostile. Few spaces outside the cultural centers and student of color-oriented spaces recognize and respect the strength and resilience these students have gained from their experiences.

Student affairs educators can be informed rather than incredulous that students gain strength from the resistance they experience. It is not an accident that these students are thriving, or that they made it to and through college. They are not anomalies. Their paths may differ from what educators may identify as traditional (e.g., college track in high school), but the words describing their experiences show that there are other ways to get a higher education. It is a way that recognizes that their strength comes from their pasts. It is not about forgetting where they are from or running from that place. It is about using the strength gained from their pasts to create a future of their choosing.

THE INFLUENCE OF OTHERS' LOW EXPECTATIONS

In addition to the themes of strength that emerge from the love of others, love for others that builds character, and the strength-building power of adversity, another theme is the influence of others' low expectations. These abhorrently low expectations—often freely expressed by teachers, classmates, and other perpetrators—derive from stereotypes about the fellows' race, cultural heritage, or the area where they grew up. Stories abound about the cultural marginalization and deeply painful messages communicated to them because of their differences. No one expected them to make it because they were from the 'hood. Many believed that school was wasted on them because they would never use their schooling to its fullest potential.

I come from a place where in school
I wasn't expected to even speak well
and that was what made me
want to show them.
–Jessie Cordova

In spite of those messages, and sometimes because of them, many fellows express a determination to make it, to get out, to achieve more than the dominant culture expects of them and to live up to the communal expectations of their own cultures.

I was raised in a society that
saw me as a waste of time…
—Susana Hernandez

Similar to the *both/and* dynamic of love and loving described above, the fellows express a second *both/and* dynamic in the ways that home and culture, the source of the unjust criticism from the dominant culture, sustained them through adversity and the roar of low expectations. They talked about the pride they felt when they returned home to hear the comments about the turns their lives had taken. The pride in being the one who got out, the one in college, the one who was going to achieve her or his dream.

But of course, they know me as the college girl.
—Kimberly Herrera

The dichotomies of their lives took many forms: contradictions of home and dominant culture, the struggles and triumphs of challenge and support, the low expectations of others inverted into high expectations for self. In their narratives, one can read their refusal to be stopped by others' depictions of who they are and what they can achieve.

I am from the ghetto—where crackheads
walk the streets and gunshots are normal.
I am from a culture rich in tradition,
with large festivals, music and tortillas....
I am the underdog that was kicked and then asked,
why don't you have anything?
I am from hope for a better tomorrow
and the promise of a brand-new day.
I am the dream.
–Darrell A. Rodriguez

To read the narratives in either an overly positive or overly negative way is to miss the essence of who the fellows are. Any stereotype—whether positive (these students are all wonderful because they have overcome adversity) or negative (students with difficult backgrounds can never succeed)—is dehumanizing because it fails to consider the individual. As student affairs educators who work with the whole of who students are, we cannot focus only on the students' pain and adversity or on the joy of their successes. The fellows do not view their lives in this one-dimensional way. Their writing is more descriptive than accusatory, more triumphant than depressed, and more inspired than downtrodden. Frank and raw in places, the narratives provide remarkable insights into how racism, classism, and sexism have affected the fellows' lives. But the narratives are simultaneously stories of how the fellows refuse to allow these "isms" to be *all* of their lives.

So What, Now What? Implications for Practice

Higher education professionals can transform their organizations and cultures to become places that recognize the strength, challenge and support, love and loving, and sense of place expressed by the MUFP fellows. Students of color, like all students, have an inherent right to their space in higher education. They have an inherent right to express their voices, cultures, and ways of being. Those who work in colleges and universities must open more space so that knowledge, theories, and voices not accepted within the academy can be fully expressed and heard. Often this means simply getting out of the way rather than granting permission; permission which is not ours to grant. Student affairs educators can suspend judgment to hear voices that may not be objective. They can entertain ideas that fly in the face of existing theory and/or comprehend impressions that shatter assumptions about proper practice.

Power and privilege in higher education have created a reality and a way of operating that can deny students their rightful space. Our rules and regulations for discipline, community standards, and facilities use intended to protect and teach can also limit and restrict. As student affairs becomes more professional and specialized, we need to make sure that what we believe we know does not hinder our openness to new ideas. This is particularly the case when we are working with students from cultures, backgrounds, or experiences different from our own.

Student affairs educators have the skills, desire, and opportunities to ensure that the voices and cultures of students like the MUFP fellows are not denied in tangible and intangible ways. Student affairs educators can be intentional to create spaces where students can express their experience, strength, and richness. When these spaces are denied, the richness of what all students have to say goes unexpressed. The narratives clearly point to ways in which those spaces can be created, nurtured, and sustained.

CHAPTER 9

Truths, Untruths, and Checking the Box

Where I'm from, contradiction blessed the ground.
–Anonymous

U sing words and expressions that often go un- or under-expressed in the student affairs literature, the "Where I Am From" narratives put forward, complex approaches to bi-culturalism, multi-culturalism, and cultural pluralism. For generations prior to the Minority Undergraduate Fellows Program (MUFP) fellows, mandatory mono-raciality was the norm. The "one-drop rule" ("any known African ancestry renders one Black" (López, 1996, p. 27)) and miscegenation (i.e., interracial marriage) laws made it legally impossible to describe oneself as "multi-racial." While multi-racial categories are now used by the U.S. Census Bureau and at colleges and universities, campus approaches to race do not fully convey all the colors, shapes, and textures of identity reflected in the narratives.

REFUSING TO CHECK ONE BOX

In the face of any lingering cultural and societal push toward mono-raciality, MUFP fellows who are multi-racial vehemently proclaim that they will not limit their identities to one expression of race, ethnicity, or culture. Without excuses, they clearly state their pride and understanding of their many, multiple, rich identities. Their approach to their ancestries reflects an open, *both/and* (e.g., multi-raciality) not an either/or (e.g., mono-raciality) perspective on race and culture, even if society still pushes them toward the latter.

> *I am not from one place.*
> *I am from Texas, Brazil, and France.*
> *I am from Bangladesh and Puerto Rico.*
> *I am from America.*
> *I am from a place that stresses*
> *a singular identity, a place*
> *that always labels me a foreigner.*
> *–Rebecca Hossain*

Reading these narratives, one can understand why so many students of color chafe against or resist "checking one box." They do not choose one identity over another; instead, they embrace *all* their identities and gain strength born of an intact cultural identity. The narratives express an approach to identity that incorporates the struggles and pain they have endured. These students express a splendid simultaneousness—they are at the same time here *and* there, they are this *and* that, they are *both/and*.

> They are the teenagers that put their
> lives on the front lines
> so I could grow up free and safe.
> They are the ones who left all they knew and loved
> in order for my life to be filled with opportunity.
> –Adiam Tesfay

In their narratives, the MUFP fellows express the ways in which they live in the whole of their experiences as cultural beings. Their refusal to "check off one box" is a metaphor for their willingness to embrace all their identities and the ambiguity that comes with that choice. In contrast to the "check one box" or "one drop rule" mono-raciality encouraged in U.S. culture, the narratives express the ways in which MUFP fellows face their identities and the opposition to their resistance. They know where they came from and are willing to do the work, again and again, of redefining their identities in a fluid, organic way. These students are connected to a larger perspective than the one discussed in older theories of diversity and multi-culturalism.

*Trying diligently to live up to the call in a place that
doubts me and allows me to be
only one or mark "other."*
–Jessica Barron

The narratives tell us something that is strikingly different from what many of us may have learned previously. You can be unified and have many identifies; you can be whole while embracing multiple identities; you do not have to choose. These students will *not* choose; to choose means rejecting one part for another.

I'm from a place where I won't choose
–LaTasha Smith

None of the fellows described situations in which they occupied the pre-encounter stage so often cited in the literature (Cross, 1971, 1978, 1985; Helms, 1990). None of the fellows talked about a time when they identified with or wished to be part of the dominant (i.e., White) culture, thus rejecting and denying their own culture.

*I will not choose my African ancestry without
explaining my native ancestry. I live in America
without embracing America. I am black,
Cherokee, and Choutou.*
–LaTasha Smith

Even as they struggled to balance their multiple selves, none of the students expressed a desire to be in a place of "passing" or denial. The MUFP fellows' experiences are different from those of previous immigrants, who were forced to give up their languages and cultural heritages. The students who were immigrants described that experience differently from how it appears in school history books. These students differ from previous generations in their multi-raciality and their willingness to live that cultural process as fully as possible.

WHOLENESS AND MULTIPLICITY

The MUFP fellows describe the richness and wholeness that stems from cultural strength, pride, and self-determination. But despite the overwhelming presence in these narratives of a perspective of wholeness, the United States (and the student affairs field as part of that culture) has not yet created enough places where people can live fully in that whole of the multiple. The MUFP fellows are clearly telling us that this is a role for college campuses.

> *I am from a place where I am taught that*
> *to be accepted I must deny the many cultures*
> *that make me, me.*
> *–Rebecca Hossain*

"Multiple" is the key word here. The narratives express the ways that the multiple approach to a many-identified existence means you do not approach your identities as discrete parts to be picked and chosen over. Rather, it is about the beautiful combination of all identities—the unique combination that makes a whole person. Whether they are writing about their own or their family's culture of origin or the one adopted through immigration, the fellows describe a wholeness and richness that results from multiple identities.

> *I am a female who constantly redefines her identity;*
> *I am black; I am African-American; I am black,*
> *I am an AMERICAN, right?*
> *—Aretha Perry*

> *When I look at myself in the mirror, I see myself in*
> *shades. Much like shades of color, my shades come in*
> *identities. My identities allow me to understand me.*
> *—Adam-Jon Aparicio*

This is a new authentic; the "authentic of the multiple." Their words encourage student affairs educators to rethink the terms "bi-cultural" and "multi-cultural." Educators have used the latter term for years with a very different meaning than what some MUFP fellows express in their narratives. The multi-culturalism of these MUFP fellows is an intra-multi-culturalism; not an inter-multi-culturalism.

Identities and cultures are not discrete, separate entities. Bi-culturalism is not an either/or proposition but a *both/and* proposition, where identities inform one another to express a whole, unique person. Many MUFP narratives show student affairs educators that the original identity development theories do not sufficiently describe the experiences of today's students. The older theories talk about identity as parts of a whole rather than the whole itself. These students are the totality of their experiences. Their lives are enriched by holding onto the wholeness of those experiences as they go forward. The MUFP fellows suggest that the idea is to think in terms of "all of the above," where the whole is greater than the sum of its parts.

> *I may live in separate worlds that may not meet today*
> *or tomorrow but they have made me who I am.*
> *–Jessica Barron*

As expressions of the whole, nothing is discarded as the fellows describe the fluidity with which they switch, change styles, and use their identities in different contexts. Generally, they respect the knowledge of their traditions, multiple languages, and heritages as they live out their lives in traditional and non-traditional ways. But the decision not to choose just one identity is not undertaken without struggle.

> *I am Hyphenated-America where I must learn to bal-*
> *ance and not just assume*
> *that everyone will have tolerance.*
> *–Ivania Hernandez*

The narratives are full of accounts of fellows' clashes with culturally traditional parents, judgments about relatives who surrendered their language and culture, sadness over their lack of native language proficiency, and deep-seated struggles to live the whole of their cultural identities in a society that asks them to check one box. When they did discuss the pain of abandoning cultural identity, it was often to express disappointment or criticism that family members had made that choice.

> I am from a culture which tells me that rejecting my
> own people is not self-hatred of my race,
> but simply moving up in the world.
> –Julie J. Park

The judgments about abandoning cultural ways—"balancing on the hyphen"—and deciding how to express one's cultural identity are related to assimilation pressures. Students who are not White, middle class, and heterosexual (i.e., dominant culture) are asked to conform to the dominant culture norm.

ASSIMILATION AND UNASSIMILATION

Assimilation, past and present, looms large in several of the narratives. In particular, the fellows speak longingly of cultures that were part of them about which they know little.

> I am a Latino, proud of my heritage; yet unfamiliar
> with it because of the ripple effect of oppression that
> white America threw at my grandparents,

then my parents, and now at me.
–Adam-Jon Aparicio

They talk about a past that is part of who they are in the here and now.

I am from a history of the Long Walk,
government policy, cultural assimilation, relocation,
boarding school education, and broken promises.
–Todd Wilcox

Many fellows describe immigrant family members or ancestors who were forced to assimilate to get ahead. Assimilation was and is a survival issue in the most literal sense of the word. In reading the narratives, one hears the respect in their voices as they recognize the sacrifice and difficult choices others have made. Simultaneously, one also hears celebration that they are being given different opportunities—often by the same people who made those earlier choices. These students struggle, to the best of their ability, not to assimilate. Despite the pressure, many expressed the desire to keep or regain their culture, traditions, and language. In this struggle, they admit that they do not always know when they are assimilating.

I am from assimilation even though
I didn't know I was being assimilated.
–Cynthia Payne

Living in the United States, with its acute social constructions around race, the MUFP fellows have experienced the expectations and labeling of the dominant culture. They are aware of the lower expectations for people of color in U.S. society. This was contrasted by the higher expectations placed on them by family and community. Small wonder, then, that the students write about the push and pull of their existence as first-generation college students, first in their neighborhood to go to college, and first in their community to "make it."

> *I'm the one that's going to make it, but what is it?*
> *Then it might not be my it.*
> *—Marie Smallwood*

Untruths Taught About Themselves

Regardless of what student affairs educators do on campus to create the safe places and support necessary for surviving and thriving, these students come to college with labels given to them by others. Many have had a lifetime of messages about not being good enough, not belonging in college, and not being worthy of the money spent on them.

> *I am from where people like me are expected to not*
> *succeed; tumble and fall and act like money is all*
> *we need to get us out of our "misery."*
> *—Ivania Hernandez*

As students of color living in the United States, these fellows have been taught untruths about themselves. They have heard all the jokes, questions, and comments about where they are from, how they or their ancestors got to the country, and what is expected and not expected of them. Few of the students mention the college campus as a place of relief from that onslaught; rather, it is often an environment in which more untruths are hurled in their direction.

> *I am from a place where the question,*
> *"Are you Saddam Hussein's*
> *daughter?" never goes without a laugh.*
> *–Rebecca Hossain*

> *I am from a place where the question,*
> *"Where are you from?" can never be*
> *asked innocently because it is always asked*
> *with an expected response of some exotic land,*
> *far far away.*
> *–Julie J. Park*

They worry that college will change them—that becoming educated, getting a degree, and living in the different cultural world of college will change them in unknown ways.

> *I am from not being accepted*
> *by those that look like me.*

I am from "she acts like she's white."
–Cynthia Payne

All students struggle with the challenge of forming their identities in the context of past, present, and future. These students carry out that task in a profoundly complicated context of racism, prejudice, and pressure to assimilate.

Caught in two worlds that sometimes collide.
–Luana Mona

BORDERS, BORDER CROSSING, AND BOUNDARIES

"Border"—as a metaphor for both immigration and cultural crossings—is a prominent theme in the "Where I Am From" narratives. The borders that are straddled include the family's immigrant past and the student's first- or second-generation present; the countries where they lived or live; their student status combined with their family's position in the community of origin; the high expectations that their families hold for them and the low expectations communicated by the racism of the United States.

Many of the narrative authors intentionally ground their consciousness in the experience of border crossing. Straddling borders means that you can hold on to who you are while simultaneously moving into the future. For the MUFP fellows, that future is higher education. By conceptualizing and framing their experiences as border crossing, they do not have to abandon any part of themselves—they can take who they are across the border to the new place. They can use their identities as a foundation for the work they do in college and in the future.

The borders reflected in these narratives are not just lines that mark one place from another. The border is a fluid space, a cusp, a blended area—the *both/and* place. It is a place where the borders are not as clear as they used to be despite others' efforts to make them so. The fellows' approach to borders, race, and identity is more fluid and flexible than that of older people, including student affairs professionals, who have experienced borders as more permanent, impermeable, and harder to cross.

> *I am from a country that doesn't know where*
> *to place my experiences with blacks or whites,*
> *not understanding that they are my own.*
> *–Julie J. Park*

They are the border-crossers of their generation. They live in the "this" *and* "that" every day. They are tested as they cross the borders of race, class, gender, and culture.

> *I was born in U.S. but at times*
> *I'm treated as if I had just*
> *swam across the Rio Grande.*
> *–Susana Hernandez*

The tests come in accusations of talking "White" and questions about where they were born. They know they are being asked to act beyond their years when they serve as go-betweens for family members unfamiliar with the language or the culture of the United States or of college. They know they are spanning borders as they negotiate the unfamiliar environment of the campus. The real and metaphorical borders described in the narratives embody messages about which side of the boundary they supposedly belong, what part of their identity fits and does not fit into the college environment, and whether college is a place where they will ever belong.

The borders and boundaries that the MUFP fellows describe are permeable, usually uncertain, and always overlapping. The MUFP fellows' words remind us that these students live in a postmodern world that is faster, more connected (technologically and otherwise), and more complex than the world in which many student affairs educators grew up. But rather than facing this world with frustration, many of these students *expect* their world to be confusing. Rather than trying to decrease the complexity or reduce the ambiguity, they seem to know that this is an aspect of life with which they must deal. The past, present, and future bleed together, because students are unwilling to give up the legacy of their past for the unknown promise of the future.

The boundaries drawn (or not drawn) with families are often difficult, contested, and in flux. The students negotiate their identities (note the plural) in a fashion of their own making. Perhaps all generations have forged their own approach to how they separate from their families (if they do at all), how they manage their family relationships, and how they advance toward their futures. But most previous generations of students have not undertaken this developmental task in such a fast-paced, complex, and uncertain environment.

It is the responsibility of student affairs educators to respect students' boundaries by understanding where they come from, how their struggles may be different from those of students in the past, and how contradiction and paradox may define these students' boundaries more vividly than sureness and certainty.

LANGUAGE

Many of the MUFP fellows are children or grandchildren of immigrants. While this experience was not common among all of them (such as African American students whose families have been in the United States for generations), many fellows' lives have crossed cultural and ethnic boundaries, including the language boundary. Many are multi-lingual or know some words and phrases of their culture's original language. The mono-lingualism of the United States has meant that a number of fellows served as translators for their parents from an early age. Many fellows have had additional schooling to learn their language of origin. Many struggled with pressures from family, school, friends, and other sources regarding which language was authentically theirs. Was it their first language (English, in many cases)? Or was it the language from their culture (a language they may not have much access to or opportunity to use)? Many were caught between the language of home and the language of school.

In the United States, multi-lingualism can be perceived as a deficit rather than a strength. In the United States, mono-lingualism is seen as an asset rather than the cultural weakness it actually is. Instead of being viewed as a flexible cultural attribute that allows people to better express who they are, multi-lingualism is viewed as something to be overcome.

I walk into my grandmother's apartment
and ask her for her blessing and she tells me

"A dios te bendiga."

We eat and I speak to her in Spanglish,
both English and Spanish.

I feel right at home. This is where I'm from.
–Kimberly Herrera

I am Salt Clan, born for San Juan Pueblo,
my maternal grandparents are Towering House Clan,
and my paternal grandparents are Edgewater Clan.

Ashiihi nishli. Kinlichiinii Dine'e bashishchiin.
Kiya'aanii da' shicheii. Tabaaha' da' shinali.

This is my identity as a Navajo man
from the communities of Leupp
and Winslow, Arizona.
–Todd Wilcox

So What, Now What? Implications for Practice

Student affairs educators, too, can become conscious border-crossers—helping and urging students to develop the skills they need to negotiate the new environment while maintaining their connection to the old. Unfortunately, students will meet resistance to their efforts in this direction—from faculty, family, and even friends—but student affairs educators can provide a place where the resistance is less pressing.

A thorough understanding of the pressures and unfairness of assimilation can assist student affairs educators, particularly those who are White, to become border-crossers. Without an understanding of all the facets of assimilation, one cannot relate to students of color as they struggle with the pressures of that process. Everyone in the United States (a country of immigration and colonization) was or is subject to assimilation. Yet assimilation has always been a different process for White people, regardless of their ethnic background, than it has been for people of color. It can be argued that many racially White people gave up their ethnicity (e.g., Irish, Ukrainian, English) to "become White" and gain the privileges of that skin-color based status. In contrast, many people of color understand that survival and growth comes from holding on to the strengths that come from their cultural backgrounds.

All student affairs educators—Whites and people of color—can acquire knowledge and get in touch with their pasts to understand their relationship to assimilation. To misunderstand the pressures, dangers, and privileges of assimilation is to miss why students of color, like the MUFP fellows, struggle with this issue. Misunderstanding assimilation and the pressure to conform leads one to misinterpret, as Beverly Tatum (1997) explained "why all the Black kids [are] sitting together in the cafeteria," (p. xiii) or why professionals of color have racial caucuses at conferences, or why student affairs professionals of color have such high turnover rates at predominantly White campuses. If White student affairs professionals understand why students of color need and deserve a balance of time together and time apart, they can understand how to craft a campus that actually engages diversity rather than merely tolerates it.

The narratives teach student affairs educators why they should not expect formerly un- or underrepresented students to express gratitude for having a place at the table. Higher education in the United States is an advantage to which all have been promised access. The MUFP fellows and any other students of color should not have to be grateful for that access, especially considering the many barriers that have been placed in their paths. No one grants students of color permission to be present in higher education. It is a tragedy that any student might think that he or she is not entitled to pursue higher education, or a college diploma, or a leadership position. The college environment and society in general are enhanced by the wisdom, robustness, and cultural perspectives of these students.

How do we incorporate the wisdom, experiences, and perspectives shared by the MUFP fellows into the institution? How does student affairs practice change when we recognize that students do not choose among their identities but experience themselves in a wholeness that our practice does not account for? Rather than taking the deficit approach that assumes deficiencies in their backgrounds, previous education, or development, how can we understand the realities of these students' strengths and presence? How do we update theory to reflect the actual lives of our current students?

Theories used in practice can lag behind the real life of students by as much as 15 to 20 years. The MUFP fellows live in a postmodern world that is vastly different from that of the scholars who created student affairs theory. Student affairs educators raised with a paradigm of logic and certainty may not have questioned the limited option of checking one box or settling on one identity. The scientific paradigm of discrete entities, narrowed options, and "one best way" does not fit current students' perceptions of the world. The bedrock theories of student affairs were built for a different reality than that of students today—or, for that matter, of current student affairs educators.

One of the joys of working in student affairs is that we do not know what our students know. Student affairs educators revel in the opportunity to stay engaged intellectually and emotionally through their work with students, and they do their best work when they stay close enough to students to understand their perspectives. When educators grow distant and out of touch, they risk establishing ill-chosen or irrelevant programs, services, and policies.

These narratives give student affairs educators a window into the perspectives, needs, and approaches of an important student population. The narratives help student affairs educators better understand students. This understanding is imperative because the authors of the narratives are students of color; ultimately, it is imperative for student affairs work with all students.

REFERENCES

Cross, W. E. (1971). The Negro-to-Black conversion experience: Toward a psychology of Black liberation. *Black World, 20*(9), 13–27.

Cross, W. E. (1978). Models of psychological nigrescence: A literature review. *Journal of Black Psychology. 5*(1), 13–31.

Cross, W. E. (1985). Black identity: Rediscovering the distinction between personal identity and reference group orientation. In M. Spencer, G. Brookins, & W. Allen (Eds.), *Beginnings: The social and affective development of Black children* (pp. 144–171). Hillsdale, NJ: Erlbaum.

Cross, W. (1991). *Shades of black: Diversity in African-American identity*. Philadelphia: Temple University Press.

Helms, J. (1990). An overview of Black racial identity theory. In J. Helms (Ed.), *Black and White racial identity: Theory, research, and practice* (pp. 9–32). New York: Greenwood Press.

López, I.F.H. (1996). *White by law: The legal construction of race*. NY: New York University Press.

Tatum, B. D. (1997). *"Why are all the Black kids sitting together in the cafeteria?" and other conversations about race*. New York: Basic Books.

CHAPTER 10

Wholeness, Authenticity, and Wisdom

I am the dream.
–Darrell A. Rodriguez

COMPLEXITY, NOT CONTRADICTION

Wholeness and complexity mark the Minority Undergraduate Fellows Program (MUFP) fellows' understanding of their experiences. Their reflections on the past, present, and future; their fluid approaches to culture, language, and tradition; and their intense connections to family and community combine in a view of life as a complex process. The narratives—snapshots of lives in process—present student affairs educators with a different image of students than the ways portrayed in student affairs textbooks. Like the case studies in those textbooks, the narratives illustrate psychosocial development. But the complexity and richness expressed in the narratives is lost in the textbooks, where developmental theory is distilled into concise statements or theoretical models. Textbooks, given their form and purpose, are bound to lose the poetry and fullness of the narratives. In the textbooks, the students' voices fade into the background, and theoretical language cannot fully capture the rich texture of their lives. We need the textbooks and the theory, but student affairs educators also need the narratives. Without access to both, the theory and the real, student development theorists and student affairs educators can inadvertently misinterpret the lives of the students.

The complexity that the fellows' describe in these narratives is an essential element of their lives. The fellows often include both sides of conflicting sentiments in their views of themselves: "I am the dream" *and* "I am the stereotype." While some might see statements like these as irreconcilable contradictions, the fellows do not define their experiences as contradictory. Contradictions are puzzles outside of or separate from one's existence. The experiences of these fellows, with all their complexities, are the essence of who they are and who they are becoming. Their journeys entail development and identity formation. The full richness of those journeys is lost if theory reconstructs the fellows' experiences as contradiction rather than complexity. Although the difference is subtle, the distinction is important.

I come from a single-parent home
and am proud and happy of it.
I would not be the person I am
if it were any other way.
I come from a place that taught me
you could be down but never out
—a place where you looked out for each other.
–Jessie Cordova

INTERNALIZED OPPRESSION

Racially conscious, critical practitioners cannot help but recognize and share the pain inflicted when young people or people of any age believe the stereotypes hurled their way. Internalized oppression is certainly in effect when students question their worthiness to be in college, are uncertain about whether they will make it, and have doubts about their talents. But those same critical practitioners must raise questions about who gets to label the fellows as suffering from internalized oppression. Whose lens is being privileged in such a judgment? Whose perspective is being used to express that "awareness?" Is it the perspective of the student affairs educator or the student of color? Who gets to define racism or oppression—the student affairs educator or the student of color who had the direct experience? What do the fellows' narratives express about their experiences? When students do not interpret their experiences the way student affairs educators do, who decides?

Many MUFP fellows, like many people of color, are prepared as much as possible by their families and home communities for the racism they will encounter. Messages about worthiness, strength, and love are delivered in ways that will, hopefully, sustain them through the onslaught of insults and low expectations they will doubtless encounter. But regardless of these acts of love, internalized oppression is bound to have its effects.

The college campus is filled with messages that add to the burden of internalized oppression. Well-intentioned programs that target students of color (regardless of their definitions of themselves), fellow classmates with underdeveloped knowledge about privilege, and faculty and administrators who have done little work in the area of social justice and oppression combine to deliver daily salvos.

As one reads the narratives, one sees a world occupied by the fellows that may not be visible to those in the dominant culture. How can these students hold such contradictory beliefs about themselves? How can they have experienced such cultural insults and come out intact? How can we use the narratives to better understand their experiences and craft a different kind of cultural experience in student affairs? Student affairs educators cannot paternalistically place themselves between the dominant culture and the students of color, but they can make a difference.

THE COMPLEXITY OF HOPE AND LACK OF HOPE

It would be a misinterpretation of the narratives to read them as pain rather than triumph, as defeat rather than victory. The narratives describe hope born of experience; experience in which the students are both the object and subject of hope.

126

They are the recipients of hope from their parents, siblings, communities, and people who believe in them.

> *I'm trying to be a role model to underprivileged,*
> *undereducated, and overlooked youth. I'm trying to*
> *be a woman that my younger sister*
> *and niece can look up to.*
> *–Lesley-Ann Brown*

> *I am from a group of kids, playing in the street*
> *who dared to dream,*
> *and went on to feel failure and success.*
> *–Andrew Villanueva*

The narratives also reflect the fellows' own hopes for the future and for themselves. Hope drives them as they aspire to a life with more opportunity than many of those around them have experienced.

> *I am not today...I am TOMORROW!*
> *–Lesley-Ann Brown*

When one combines the hope instilled in the fellows with the love and faith of the communities they are from, it is possible to see why they are so determined to persevere. While hopefulness is generally the purview of the young, the hope expressed in the narratives is of a greater magnitude. One has to admire

the faith these students have in the benefits of higher education, the tenacity with which they pursue their dreams, and the
conviction with which they believe in their futures.

But while hope is abundant in the narratives, lack of hope
also emerges as a theme. Some of them experienced lack of hope
when they entered college, because people neither expected nor
welcomed them. The barriers placed in front of them in the form
of money, language, attitude, and prejudice communicated that
they were not supposed to have hope. In the face of the messages that communicated this lack of hope, the fellows experienced
success.

> *I am from persistence to prove I could*
> *do more than others believed...*
> *Fear and overcoming it,*
> *from hope and pride and endurance.*
> *–Briza Juarez*

PERSEVERANCE

A number of the narratives speak to the idea that expressing
hope comes from holding onto oneself and believing that things
are going to be okay. Generally, the fellows believe that if one has
faith in oneself and in one's culture, one will make it, in spite of
(or because of) the struggles endured. It is about perseverance,
about keeping at it with the faith that "this" (whatever "this" is)
will change. Their approach is a mixture of hope, leaps of faith,
and a belief that they can make a difference.

To persevere, the fellows turn adversity into triumph, creativity, dreams, hope, and strength. Like the threads in a tapestry, it is hard to tell where one experience ends and another begins. The tough times are not "snags" in the tapestry but part of the pattern. This transformation of negative into positive does not come without a cost. One can read the pain, abandonment, and confusion in the fellows' words. But the narratives can teach us to go beyond multi-cultural theory that emphasizes disadvantage. The multi-cultural theory grounded in the narratives is about the strength and hope that comes from difficult experiences and backgrounds. There is wisdom in the pain of coming from the experiences they describe.

The fellows come from places very different from college. A common theme in the narratives is that of using skills and knowledge from a former place (home) in the new place (college). The fellow's skills and knowledge were forged under difficult circumstances and include strength, hope, complexity, and wholeness. The problem is that these skills and this knowledge may not be recognizable to many on the college campus. How can student affairs educators make the campus and its members more multi-vocal, multi-aural, and multi-skilled? How can student affairs educators work not to change the fellows or other students into people who look and sound like them, but to change the environment so the skills and knowledge of the fellows are recognized as legitimate ways of being? How can their experiences shape our practice?

I am from senseless black-on-brown violence. RIP
T-shirts, racial profiling, smog, murdered friends,
wounded loved ones, a virtual black tunnel with a
bright light at the end for those who dare to dream
past high school graduation.
—Andrew Villanueva

The fellows show their perseverance even as they describe the ways in which they are not taken seriously by others. There is no "poor me" in their stories. They write of praying to withstand the storms they will encounter. They know the futility of trying to avoid the hard times, yet they express surprisingly little bitterness about the inevitable difficulties. They are not angry that something bad happened or that something good did not happen. Their view of life is not romanticized. Many understand the wholeness gained from embracing the good and the bad.

I am from…
Persistence to prove
I could do
more than others believed.
—Briza Juarez

In their narratives, the fellows simultaneously acknowledge and defy the limits placed on them. They depict powerful examples of the ways in which they stand firmly in defiance of those who do not believe they should be here—whether the "here" is college, success, or anywhere else they choose to be. The fellows tell stories filled with the ways in which they claim space, rise above, and overcome. They are determined to make something for themselves and their families.

Toughness, Wisdom, and Groundedness

The narratives can help student affairs educators understand resilience born of struggle. Many fellows have experienced more than their share of pain in their young lives, but the narratives do not dwell on the negative. Pain and struggle are mentioned along with toughness—pain made them stronger; struggle made them who they are. To these students, pain and struggle are realities, a life experience.

I am from anger, resentment, pain, hurt,
tradition, culture, hate, abuse, religion, sacrifice, love,
but most of all, I am from THIS world.
—Candace Nikki Rogers

The wholeness, authenticity, and wisdom expressed in the narratives reveal a powerful presence. Through struggle, difficult choices, and painful decisions, the students are building strong identities. The narratives sing about the dreams and goals of the fellows, their families, and, in some cases, their people as a culture. Their power comes from home, family, self, survival, and faith. It is grounded in the commitment of the people who sacrificed for them, worked hard to provide, and hung together to give them a better life. Their power comes from the truths told about them in the context of home and family. It emanates from their cultures, people, histories, and backgrounds. The racial identity and student development theories of student affairs do not adequately capture the richness, wholeness, and power that come from knowing one's culture.

The fellows are taught that difficulty is inevitable but that they are strong enough to overcome it. They know that some people will try to put them down, but they do not have to accept that. They know that some people will hate them, but in the context of home and family, there is love.

> *I am loved and protected by many*
> *I am judged and ridiculed*
> *by those who don't know me*
> *I have been blessed by God,*
> *yet am being chased by the devil*
> *I have confidence that one day we will all*
> *walk on clouds and not be burdened*
> *I am finding out more about myself from others.*
> *—E. K. Lewis*

In the same short narrative, struggle, wisdom, and toughness are in juxtaposition. Often in the same sentence, fellows talk about the good and bad parts of their homes, childhoods, and current lives.

> *I am from being accepted the most*
> *by the ones that I "act" like*
> *—but only accepted the most—not completely,*
> *But, I am from love, support, discipline,*

dominance and privilege.
I am from the blessings of God.
On a lighter note...
–Cynthia Payne

Wholeness and wisdom are communicated in their stories of survival and achievement, pain and joy. Many fellows know that life is not easy. Many do not expect life, college, or the future to be easy. But to read the "Where I Am From" narratives for the pain and overlook the dreams and hopes is to miss the meaning.

RUNNING TO, NOT FROM

With their feet firmly planted in the past, the fellows are living in the present, and, simultaneously, aimed at the future. They are propelled, inspired, and motivated about their futures while their individual and cultural histories inform that forward motion. In keeping with their complex *both/and* approach to life, they are looking ahead *and* remembering where they came from.

Ready and willing, self-conscious
and awkward, unique
and unconventional challenged
by the challenging and hopeful for tomorrow.
–Jessica Barron

College and university educators assume that some students attend college to escape from or "get out" of an untenable situation. The fellows' often reflective, usually warmhearted accounts

133

of their pasts do not describe running from or trying to escape from anything. Instead, like other students, they went to college to expand their choices, develop skills to get a better job, and improve their opportunities, among other reasons. Possibly more than most students, many fellows have turned adversity into strength. In this transformative process, their past grounds and inspires them. The past is an important place to work from, not a place to forget or run away from.

For many MUFP fellows, college attendance is not an exposure to a completely new way of life; they've already made certain choices about how they want to live, just as anyone would. They speak about reaching, teaching, helping, and being helped. They can go home again if they want to. They can move to a vastly different kind of place. Or they can choose something in between. Whatever they do, choice is essential. Whatever they do, choice is essential. They have the choice to adopt or refuse to adopt a middle-class lifestyle; the choice to remain in or return to their home communities; the choice to go elsewhere in search of their futures. It is about where they want to be, not where someone thinks they should be. For all students who pursue higher education, regardless of their social class, student affairs educators can visualize different ways of being beyond middle-class socialization. The hope is that these students have a choice to enter the class and lifestyle of their choosing and not be subject to an automatic, predetermined choice made by someone else.

In this book, we advocate the tried-and-true student affairs approach of starting where the student is. More than ever, the practice of respecting what students (particularly students of color) bring with them from their pasts is essential. Our role is to provide campus experiences that recognize and acknowledge what students carry with them from their pasts so they can use those gifts as assets in their futures.

So What, Now What? Implications for Practice

How do these themes of complexity, hope, and perseverance inform our work as student affairs educators? Because the narratives strikingly contradict many standard student affairs understandings about race and class, how can student affairs educators use them to better understand students? The role of student affairs educators is to learn about the cultures and backgrounds of students like the MUFP fellows so we can understand how they approach their lives from the point of view of strengths and assets. "Assets" refers to all the parts of a student's life—the resources accrued from background, culture, and history; and the unique approach with which that student will navigate the higher education environment. The narratives provide a window into the strengths and assets of these students. They serve as a beginning, not an end, for that exploration. A respectful approach to understanding students' lives entails asking questions, reading theory and biography, and placing yourself in cultural situations different from your own.

Multi-culturalism, if viewed from a "deficit" or "disadvantage" perspective, can give the impression that students of color are blank slates on which student affairs educators need to write a more "advantaged" culture (i.e., an educated one). This disadvantage perspective assumes that students like the MUFP fellows are cultural beings whose disadvantages need to be overcome. The "Where I Am From" narratives defy this depiction.

Student affairs plays a significant role in helping students become more conscious of what they want from their education and their lives. During the past 10 years, student affairs has led campus efforts about multi-culturalism and cultural pluralism. With an enhanced understanding of race and class from an assets perspective, student affairs can continue to lead campus efforts on fairness and social justice.

On and off campus, student affairs educators make a commitment to creating classrooms and environments that recognize wisdom born of experience. Student affairs educators can participate with the fellows and other students to deepen our understanding of the way we construct environments that are more inclusive and open to the experiences of others. The approach advocated in this book—reading the "whole" of students' lives—calls for professionals to be conscious of what students bring to the campus. This approach calls for student affairs educators to understand the ways in which students' experiences enrich the campus community simply by bringing all of who they are to the campus.

The narratives teach us to listen to the wisdom that students express about their lives. They teach us not to be complacent about what we think we know. They teach us to listen to the wisdom and beauty of students' lives. This wisdom goes back to the discussion about how graduate education and theory can distance us from what we know. Regardless of the strengths of the student affairs curriculum, the benefits of graduate preparation, and the importance of a firm foundation in the theoretical and practical bases of our field, we need to stay grounded in the wisdom and beauty of students' lives.

CHAPTER 11

The Final "So What, Now What?" Implications for Practice

The original purpose of the "Where I Am From" exercise was to link the Minority Undergraduate Fellows Program (MUFP) fellows' past (e.g., history, culture, family background) and present (e.g., college knowledge, development and growth) experiences. This book provides a forum, a gathering of voices, for the MUFP fellows' narratives. As the narratives were written over several Student Leadership Institutes it became clear that they could teach student affairs educators lessons that theories have not captured. The purpose of the

137

"Where I Am From" exercise was expanded to read and discuss the narratives in ways that saw the whole of these students' lives. A goal of the book was to broaden the response repertoire of student affairs professionals through a consideration of the themes within the stories of the narratives. We, Susan Borrego and Kathleen Manning, hope to add to the literature in ways that change practice. These fellows *are* the change that the student affairs field needs to see. We hope the readers of this book will transform higher education by considering the following:

+ Student affairs educators have the opportunity and ability to transform colleges and universities into places that recognize the strengths of students, especially students of color.

+ If student affairs educators suspend their judgment about what they believe they know about students' lives, new doors will open for practice and education.

+ Much of what is discussed in this book involves how power and privilege are structured in higher education institutions.

+ Theory is a remarkable tool in student affairs practice, but only when it is used judiciously and not as a replacement for the truth about students' lives.

+ We rarely know all there is to know about students' experiences or their dreams for the future.

✦ Students' backgrounds are an integral part of the tapestry of their lives. Particularly with students of color, cultural differences may interfere with full disclosure about the strengths and weaknesses of a person's past.

✦ Without any additional development challenge from student affairs educators, challenge for students of color—and perhaps for all students—is a major aspect of their lives.

✦ Border crossing—for both students and student affairs educators—is a powerful metaphor for the promise of our work together.

✦ Awareness of culture, our own and that of others, is an essential aspect of identity and development.

✦ Student affairs educators must have a powerful analysis of assimilation, culture, and race to do their best work with students.

✦ For students of color to truly succeed, others must learn to listen.

✦ The wisdom of students, especially students of color, is an asset higher education cannot afford to ignore.

✦ Sense of place, particularly in expressions about the places people are from, is a powerful part of being human.

✦ Any window into a student's perspective, needs, and approach to life is worthy of exploration.

✦ The wisdom contained in the narratives may contradict the wisdom expressed in the foundational theories of student affairs. Drawing knowledge from all sources is an important professional skill.

✦ While the deficit approach to multi-culturalism has long been considered passé, our practice may still be driven by some of the assumptions in those theories.

✦ Higher education can be more than training for the middle class.

✦ The aspects of place expressed in the "Where I Am From" narratives can suggest ideas for creating space on campus. Place and space create tangible experiences, memories, and identities.

Student affairs educators are blessed with the opportunity to experience students' lives. We thank the MUFP fellows for granting us the gift of sharing their experiences and worlds with us, and for allowing us to publish their narratives.